# Conducting Educational
# Needs Assessment

# Evaluation in Education and Human Services

**Editors:**

George F. Madaus, Boston College, Chestnut
  Hill, Massachusetts, U.S.A.
Daniel L. Stufflebeam, Western Michigan
  University, Kalamazoo, Michigan, U.S.A.

# Conducting Educational Needs Assessments

Daniel L. Stufflebeam

Charles H. McCormick

Robert O. Brinkerhoff

Cheryl O. Nelson

**Kluwer-Nijhoff Publishing**
**a member of the Kluwer Academic Publishers Group**

**Boston-Dordrecht-Lancaster**

Distributors for North America:
KLUWER ACADEMIC PUBLISHERS
190 Old Derby Street
Hingham, MA 02043, U.S.A.

Distributors outside North America:
KLUWER ACADEMIC PUBLISHERS GROUP
Distribution Centre
P.O. Box 322
3300 AH Dordrecht
THE NETHERLANDS

**Library of Congress Cataloging in Publication Data**
Main entry under title:

Conducting educational needs assessment.

  (Evaluation in education and human services)
  "June 1984."
  Bibliography: p.
  Includes index.
  1. Educational surveys. 2. School management
and organization—Planning. I. Stufflebeam,
Daniel L. II. Series.
LB2823.C59 1984      379.1'54      84-15466
ISBN 0-89838-160-6

# Contents

# List of Figures

# List of Tables

# Preface

What goals should be addressed by educational programs? What priorities should be assigned to the different goals? What funds should be allocated to each goal? How can quality services be maintained with declining school enrollments and shrinking revenues? What programs could be cut if necessary? The ebb and flow of the student population, the changing needs of our society and the fluctuation of resources constantly impinge on the education system. Educators must deal with students, communities, and social institutions that are dynamic, resulting in changing needs. It is in the context of attempting to be responsive to these changes, and to the many wishes and needs that schools are asked to address, that needs assessment can be useful.

Needs assessment is a process that helps one to identify and examine both values and information. It provides direction for making decisions about programs and resources. It can include such relatively objective procedures as the statistical description and analysis of standardized test data and such subjective procedures as public testimony and values clarification activities. Needs assessment can be a part of community relations, facilities planning and consolidation, program development and evaluation, and resource allocation. Needs assessment thus addresses a broad array of purposes and requires that many different kinds of procedures be available for gathering and analyzing information. This book was written with this wide variation of practices in mind.

*Conducting Educational Needs Assessment* contains six chapters and two appendixes. Chapter 1, "Introduction to Needs Assessment," provides some general information concerning relevant definitions, concepts, and practices in the area of needs assessment. Basic steps in the needs assessment process are described, and a checklist of activities for the needs assessment process is provided.

Chapters 2 through 6, explain and illustrate each important aspect of the needs assessment process. Chapter 2, "Preparation," discusses the planning and communications work that must precede and provide the foundation for the needs assessment. "Information Gathering," chapter 3, discusses the general nature of the process of collecting information and describes several specific information gathering procedures. The task of analyzing the collected information is discussed in chapter 4, and a detailed nonfiction example illustrates the process. Chapter 4 is supplemented by Appendix B, "Analysis Techniques," which includes a description, sample application, and references for other analytic procedures. Chapter 5, "Reporting the Needs Assessment Results" provides information about communications techniques, report formats and content, criteria for reporting, and graphic techniques for displaying information. In addition, some reporting examples are presented. In chapter 6, the authors discuss standards by which needs assessments can be evaluated.

*Conducting Educational Needs Assessment* is not a compendium of theoretical viewpoints or disagreements, but, rather, reflects the authors' goal of providing a useful reference to the educator involved in doing a needs assessment. The book is likely to be most useful in making one aware of the several dimensions of and approaches to needs assessment, and as a resource in planning and identifying the many tasks of a needs assessment study.

# Conducting Educational
# Needs Assessment

# 1 INTRODUCTION TO NEEDS ASSESSMENT

One year the king and queen of Timbuktu accumulated a surplus of 1,000,000 gold weebels in the castle treasury as a result of a large gold strike in the royal mines that year. Since their subjects had worked so hard in the mines to produce the gold, the king and queen came under considerable pressure to spend the surplus for the benefit of those subjects. In an attempt to reach a decision about how to spend these funds, the king and queen called a meeting of their ten most trusted advisors, who presented the following information:

1. Most of the roads in the kingdom were riddled with ruts and holes, causing the delay of commercial traffic.
2. Only six of the 25 bridges in the kingdom could withstand the weight of the recently developed heavy catapults of the army.
3. Practically all of the subjects in the kingdom wanted the royal family to sponsor a kingdom-wide festival and celebration.
4. Thirty percent of the subjects had contaminated wells that were causing their family members to become ill.
5. The moat in the southern defensive perimeter of the kingdom was shallow enough to wade across.

6. The revenues for the coming year were uncertain.

It was obvious to all involved that the surplus was not sufficient to address all of the identified problems and preferences adequately. The king and queen were confronted with a dilemma. Repairing the roads would benefit primarily the merchants and farmers who used them for commerce, but it would also increase the flow of tax revenue. Improving the bridges would increase the military response potential of the army but would disrupt the transportation of commercial goods. A kingdom-wide celebration would be most enjoyable and would put the king and queen in favorable light with their subjects. However, their current relations with their subjects were good. New wells would improve the health and productivity of their subjects. However, some advisors voiced concern about providing resources directly to individual families and felt that this was not the royal family's responsibility. The defensibility of the moat in the southern part of the kingdom was of concern to the king and queen as the relations with the tribes who lived south of the kingdom were constantly strained. Finally, the uncertainties about the coming year's income led them to consider the possibility of doing nothing with the surplus in the treasury until the finances for the coming year were more certain.

Thus, the king and queen were given several competing options representing different values and desires. During a meeting, their advisors presented rationales for each option, and at least two advisors were adamant in their support of each option.

The king and queen were disappointed that there were no obvious "winners" among the competing choices, which would have simplified their decision-making. Clearly a much more in-depth, careful analysis was needed. However, they were scheduled to leave for a vacation the next day and were not willing to delay their departure. Therefore, they chose an expedient approach and decided to expend the surplus on the first two items drawn from a hat—a fair, but by no means analytic method. By this method, the road improvement program and kingdom-wide festival were chosen. Unfortunately, during the rulers' vacation, the tribes to the south of the kindgom attacked across the shallow moat at the southern defensive perimeter. The kingdom was taken over in three short days of warfare.

Moral of the story: it pays to analyze one's priorities carefully before going on vacation.

The preceding example, though obviously fictitious and oversimplified, is analogous to situations in education when needs assessment is relevant. A needs assessment offers a rational approach to determining priorities and allocating resources. Many factors that one could encounter in a real educational needs assessment are evident in the story of the king and queen. First, there are seldom enough resources to address all identified needs adequately, especially since most educational funds have been previously encumbered and are not readily available for new needs. Second, the availability of resources for the future is often uncertain, making long-term commitments and planning difficult. Third, many needs are worthy and defensible and hence are in competition for limited resources. Fourth, decision-makers must make decisions about diverse kinds of needs which represent different values, beliefs, and philosophies and are, therefore, generally difficult to compare. Fifth, decisions are often made rapidly and under stressful conditions that prohibit the gathering or careful analysis of all desired information. While there are certainly additional factors that effect educational needs assessment, those cited above provide a flavor for the general difficulties one may encounter when implementing a needs assessment.

This book presents a rational approach to program planning and improvement through needs assessment. It is intended to assist the practitioner in identifying and managing the many factors that impinge on educational decision-making and program improvement. The book has two major purposes: first, to provide the reader with appropriate background information and concepts relating to needs assessment; second, to present a flexible approach to educational needs assessment that will help the practitioner prepare, implement, interpret, and evaluate a needs assessment study.

The remainder of chapter 1 is comprised of two sections. First, some general observations are offered regarding the practice of needs assessment, current needs assessment literature, and ongoing theoretical and practical problems in the field of needs assessment. Second, the authors suggest how need can be defined and how needs assessment can be conceptualized to avoid the attendant problems.

## The Current Practice of Needs Assessment

The concept of needs assessment evolved in the mid-1960s as a direct offshoot of the social action legislation of the period. Assessments of need were often required as a basis for program goals and the level of funding requested to address those goals. Since that time, needs assessment has expanded in purpose, practice, and utilization in education. Needs assessments are used to address most areas of educational programming and student growth (such as academic, emotional, social, vocational aesthetic, physical, and moral) (Stufflebeam, 1977) at local, state, regional, and national levels. Needs assessments are implemented for several reasons; two primary reasons are to assist in planning and to promote effective public relations. Other purposes include identifying and diagnosing problems and assisting in the evaluation of the merit and worth of a program or other endeavor. Thus, it is a process that can be used for many different purposes.

If one were to review a random sample of all needs assessment reports, a major observation would be their diversity in scope, focus, and methodology. Consider, for example, a needs assessment concerning the physical skills of high school students in a single district using the results from a physical fitness test. Compare this to a needs assessment addressing all areas of student growth for special education students within a multidistrict special education unit. The diversity to be encountered in needs assessment reports is readily apparent given just these contrasting examples.

The current practice of needs assessment can be summarized as follows:

1. It has increased in popularity and utilization over the last two decades.
2. It is a highly diverse process.
3. It is an endeavor that occurs in almost every level and area of education.
4. It serves many purposes but is used primarily for planning and public relations.

## Current Needs Assessment Literature

In the professional educational literature, needs assessment tends to be included under the broader heading of program evaluation (Kaufman, 1972; Stufflebeam, 1977; Scriven and Roth, 1978). Needs assessment and evaluation involve many of the same measurement and analysis techniques. Also, both needs assessment and evaluation involve identifying and ranking the importance of problems and examining the effectiveness and worth of programs and services in relationship to the problems they are intended to address.

Perhaps the major distinction is in the temporal perspective of a needs assessment versus an evaluation study. Needs assessments usually (but not always) address a future-oriented question—what goals could or should a program or service be pursuing? Evaluation, on the other hand, usually (but again not always) addresses a present- or past-oriented question—what has the program achieved?

When reviewing the literature on needs assessment, one encounters an array of confusing terms. A detailed discussion of the differences and relationships among these terms is not likely to be helpful when it comes to actually doing a needs assessment. What may be more useful is to consider the actual practice of needs assessment and to summarize some basic approaches to identifying needs.

Stufflebeam (1977) has attempted to clarify and summarize different approaches and definitions and some of the advantages and disadvantages associated with each (see table 1-1). Table 1-1 includes four general views of the needs assessment process and lists some of the advantages and disadvantages that may be associated with each view.

The first approach identified by Stufflebeam is the *discrepancy view*, which is best characterized by the work of Kaufman (1972). It is probably the most popular approach to needs assessment. In this view, a need is a discrepancy or gap between measures or perceptions of desired performance and observed or actual performance, and herein lies a major potential problem. It is often applied in situations where norms and standards are readily available and where measurable criteria are emphasized. Particular examples are testing programs in which norm-referenced instruments are used and situations in which percentage of objectives achieved or accreditation standards are used. It may also include the use of measurement techniques such as opinionnaires in which arbitrary criteria are set in relationship to highly subjective data. The discrepancy view is generally accepted by school districts and state and federal education agencies.

This approach has several disadvantages, however. Discrepancy studies avoid the less easily measured areas. The validity of the performance standards, pronouncements of accrediting agencies, or concensual ratings tend to be accepted on face value and their social or educational value often goes unanalyzed. This approach also tends to reduce needs assessment to a simplistic, mechanical process of comparing quantifiable observations or perceptions to standards or criteria and describing the resulting gaps. Thus, the discrepancy approach may limit the needs assessment process to a consideration of achievements, products, or output to the exclusion of assessments of inputs or processes.

A familiar approach identified by Stufflebeam is the *democratic view*, which is derived more from the practice than from the theory of needs assessment. In this approach, need is defined as a change or direction desired by a majority of some reference group. This approach can be used

Table 1-1.  Advantages and Disadvantages Accruing from Different Definitions of Need

| Definitions | Advantages | Disadvantages |
|---|---|---|
| *Discrepancy view*: A need is a discrepancy between desired performance and observed or predicted performance. | Is highly amenable to the use of norm-referenced and criterion-referenced tests as well as certification checklists<br><br>Is generally accepted by school districts and state education departments | Tends to concentrate needs assessment studies on those variables for which tests and norms are available<br><br>Oversimplifies the criterion problem by attributing more validity than is deserved to norms, arbitrary standards, and pronouncements by accrediting agencies<br><br>Tends to reduce needs assessment to a simplistic mechanical process |
| *Democratic view*: A need is a change desired by a majority of some reference group. | Has high public relations value<br><br>Is equitable in considering diverse perspectives<br><br>Tends to consider a wide range of variables<br><br>Involves many people in the goal-setting process<br><br>Provides useful information for determining the relative importance of potential needs<br><br>Is easy to apply | Confuses needs with preferences<br><br>Depends heavily on the extent that the reference group is informed<br><br>Tends to confound needs determinations with cost and comfort considerations<br><br>Admits very real possibilities of forming invalid goals |

| | | |
|---|---|---|
| *Analytic view*: A need is the direction in which improvement can be predicted to occur, given information about current status. | Exalts informed judgment and systematic problem solving<br>Seeks full and complete description<br>Focuses on improvement as opposed to remediation<br>Does not depend on a priori statements of standards | Is an abstraction that may be difficult to operationalize<br>Requires highly skilled personnel |
| *Diagnostic view*: A need is something whose absence or deficiency proves harmful. | Assumes that survival needs will not be overlooked<br>Provides for the identification of met and unmet needs<br>Uses logic and available research evidence to ascertain what deficiencies would be harmful<br>Is amenable to the checklist approach | Concentrates on basic survival needs to the exclusion of higher order needs<br>Concentrates on removing the harmful effects of deprivation to the exclusion of seeking ways to improve on practice and performance that are already satisfactory<br>Is highly subjective in practice, since research in education provides little evidence about the effects of various kinds of educational deprivation<br>Is based on the questionable assumption that some needs are absolute |

to involve many people in the needs assessment process and, therefore, has high public relations value. It can be applied quite easily and can be used to sample opinion regarding a wide range of variables and potential needs. It presents, however, several drawbacks. A major problem is that the democratic view can easily confuse needs and preferences. The degree to which members of the reference groups are adequately informed will affect how they respond. Analytic information will likely be sacrificed to more immediate, observable variables related to cost or comfort. The perceived needs as determined by a majority vote may be the most popular, but may not be the most valid, given other needs information such as an analysis of the causes of current problems.

A third approach identified by Stufflebeam is the *analytic view*, in which a need is described as the direction in which improvement can be predicted to occur, given information about current status. It is future-oriented and involves critical thinking about trends and problems that may arise. It addresses such broad questions as "What skills must our graduates have to compete successfully in the work setting?" For example, students entering school today will need computer literacy and awareness to compete in the job market. This approach is characterized by an emphasis on informed judgment, systematic in-depth problem analysis, and the full and complete description of a situation. It focuses on the broad improvement of performance rather than on the remediation of performance in selected areas of deficiency. It does not depend on the establishment of singular standards of satisfactory performance but rather posits the existence of multiple, interrelated standards for the assessment of needs. An example of this approach would be the convening of a blue ribbon panel of educational futurists to consider and identify the educational problems and priorities of the next 50 years such as the assimilation of computers and other technology into the educational system. A major problem with this approach is that it may be difficult to implement, given its comprehensiveness and its dependence on skilled and qualified people.

In the fourth approach, the *diagnostic view*, need is defined as something whose absence or deficiency proves harmful or whose presence is beneficial. This approach uses logic and available research to identify and describe deficiencies that may be harmful, and requires that a relationship between two variables be documented to be able to substantiate that harm or benefit results on one variable from the withholding or provision of the other variable. For example, a child diagnosed as hearing-impaired can be tested with and without a hearing aid to determine the degree of benefit resulting from use of the aid. This is one of the few instances in education where the relationship of harm or benefit can be clearly documented. If a student performs poorly on an assessment of basic science knowledge, one does not know if the cause is poor reading skills, fatigue, lack of motivation, a poor instructional program, and so on. Because the causal relationships between deprivation and harm in the context of education are difficult to establish, basic survival needs tend to be emphasized to the exclusion of higher order, more abstract needs.

There are several theoretical and practical problems of which the needs assessor should be aware. These will be discussed in the next section under the subheadings of scope, analysis, politics, and definitions.

## Problems in the Practice and Theory of Needs Assessment

### Scope

The scope of a needs assessment is defined in part by the types of needs and the systems or level(s) of a system that will be studied. To plan a needs assessment, decisions must be made about the area(s) of needs that will be studied (for example, the social, mental health, and economic needs of alcoholics; skill deficits of special education teachers; students' math skills), and the group whose needs are to be studied. Is the target group located in a neighborhood, a school building, a city, a state, a department, and so forth? Decisions regarding such parameters will help determine the scope of the needs assessment. A second dimension of scope concerns how much and what kind of information will be gathered and considered in the needs assessment process. In practice, needs assessment is usually part of a decision-making process in which three general categories of information are addressed: (1) current (or desired) performance; (2) means to maintain or achieve desired performance; and (3) cost, viability, and other information related to actions that may be recommended. Every time they design a needs assessment study practitioners must resolve the issue of what broad areas of information will be considered. The questions to be addressed must be identified before beginning a needs assessment study. This will help to insure that the necessary or desired information is collected, analyzed, and reported in a timely manner in relation to the questions to be addressed. Will the needs assessment lead only to the description of needs? Or will the need priorities and possible responses to the needs also be studied?

For example, needs assessments are often required as part of the process to develop a grant proposal and obtain funding. The directions or requirements for completing a grant application may require that certain information be collected from certain people; that the information collection and analysis process yield a rank-ordered list of needs; and that these needs be addressed in the proposed activities and budget. Usually there is a rather clear timetable for this entire process that includes not only the time for the needs assessment, but also the time it will take to write the proposal, have it approved by a local governing board, and transmit it to the appropriate agency. A useful guideline to follow in specifying the scope of a needs assessment is that the scope must be defined so that the study will yield sufficient and timely information as required by the decisions that are to be made.

### Analysis

A most perplexing problem in needs assessment is the analysis and interpretation of information. Guidelines for the criteria, standards, or processes that are adequate or effective for making judgments about needs are ultimately subjective. This is not a problem that will one day have a definitive objective solution but rather is a complex dimension of decision making. A simplistic approach to needs assessment is to use test results or some other easily quantified measure and to compare actual results to a predetermined standard such as a local or national norm or a percentage of objectives to be achieved. The difference between the observed performance and the standard is the need. The difficulty here is that such a standard is too often arbitrarily established and may have little to recommend it except its availability and ease of application. These difficulties are made clear in the following statement by A. Stafford Clayton (1965):

> Average, normal or typical performance of any kind makes no moral claim, nor any deviations from the statistical normal/abnormal in the perjorative sense. The central tendency of a distribution has nothing to recommend morally; the typical is frequently not the morally preferable. If the tyranny of the norm is to be avoided, we must avoid this variety of deriving an 'ought' for an 'is'.

In practice, little attention may be paid to the worth or value of the standard and its relationship to societal values and goals. As Guba and Lincoln (1982) have pointed out, the specification of underlying values must be an integral part of any worthwhile needs assessment. Clearly, the values basis of needs requires extensive consideration prior to doing a needs assessment.

## Politics

Another problem concerns the political aspects of needs assessment. A needs assessment can be a complex, potentially powerful, and difficult process to implement. One must keep in mind the capability a needs assessment has to affect people and resources, especially money, in order to be aware of the potential to arouse political forces. It is a process that has the potential to change or affect many different levels of a program or an organization. If not done in a balanced and careful manner, a needs assessment can give undue emphasis to particular problems, unmet needs, or goals to the exclusion or detriment of others. Such an emphasis can lead to only superficial concern for existing strengths of a program and to the conclusion that such strengths are unimportant. In another vein, a needs assessment could give undue attention to fads and other issues with high political or public relations value. Since needs assessment are sometimes used to review or modify the activities of an existing agency or program with a treatment program already in existence, the real and perceived effectiveness of an existing program and the political status of the program or agency will affect how the needs assessment is approached. Also, if not carefully controlled, a needs assessment may give unequal attention to different groups within the population of interest. Adequate needs assessment must include the identification of strengths, support for the integrity of existing worthwhile activities and fair treatment of subgroups in the society. Drastic and deep change in programs must be considered carefully over a period of time. This should reduce the likelihood that transient political or attitudinal factors lead to a drastic change in a program that is not warranted in the long view.

## Definition

As indicated above, there is no commonly accepted definition of need. It is, therefore, important that the needs assessor decide which definition will serve as a guide for a given study. The definition will have significant implications for how the study is conducted. For example, the discrepancy approach could be implemented in a skeletal fashion with only performance indicators and desired performance levels. The diagnostic definition, however, requires the determination of a level of adequacy or sufficiency of performance and the documentation of a loss or gain in that performance as a result of its relationship to another variable. By implication, the information required for a study will vary with the definition of need on which the study is based. A working definition of need is thus basic to a needs assessment study.

### Definition of Need

Our proposed definition of need is based on a standard dictionary definition of this term (*Webster's Third International Dictionary*, G & C Merriam Company, Springfield, Mass., 1976):

> A need is something that is necessary or useful for the fulfillment of a defensible purpose.

Something that is *useful* helps but may not be essential in fulfilling a purpose. A *necessary* thing is one that is required to achieve a particular purpose. A *defensible purpose* is one that meets certain evaluative criteria. The proposed definition is intentionally flexible in order to be useful in the many settings and content areas in which needs assessments occur. It also accommodates the various concepts of need found in the needs assessment literature.

This definition of need has several implications that should be recognized. Need is not equated with narrow concepts such as necessity or discrepancy. The proposed definition of need is broader than just the difference between observed and desired states of affairs (such as the discrepancy between a district's reading scores and its reading score objective) or the easily observed results when one is deprived of basic elements such as oxygen, shelter, or particular nutrients. The definition is based on the assumption that needs do not exist per se but rather are the outcomes of human judgments, values, and interactions within a given context. Need is treated as a relative and abstract concept dependent on the purpose(s) being served and on the current situation and knowledge about what may be required or desired in relation to serving a given purpose. Therefore, any needs assessment information must be judged and interpreted within the context of purposes, values, knowledge, cause-effect relationships, and so on in order to reach a decision about what constitutes a need. Even life-sustaining substances are needs only under the assumption that life should be preserved. Arguments about euthanasia illustrate the importance of this assumption. The relative nature of all needs is an assumption made in this book, and it is especially pertinent in education, because it is a field of endeavor that reflects many values of diverse communities, theories, and practices.

A key concept in the proposed definition is *defensible purpose*. It is through this concept that values and beliefs, the foundations of need, become operational. Defensible purpose, like need, must be a flexible concept. Since needs assessment can be implemented as almost any level of human or organizational endeavor, defensible purpose must likewise be defined so that the concept is useful in many situations. We approach this problem first by defining and illustrating what we mean by purpose; second by presenting the criteria we use to address defensibility; and third by considering the necessary tradeoffs between competing purposes.

Schools can address purposes such as fostering students' growth and development, transmitting the values of the culture, developing skills and attitudes to promote good citizenship, developing useful job skills, etc. A math program or department within a given school building might include fostering the development of positive attitudes towards math, helping students develop computation skills, facilitating the development of critical thinking skills, etc. The purpose for a given math course may be to provide students with the math skills necessary to be an effective consumer or to manage a checking account correctly. The definition of purpose depends on the level and nature of the system or unit under consideration.

After identifying the many purposes that a program or organizational unit could address, the defensibility of these purposes should be considered. Four types of criteria can be used to evaluate the defensibility of purposes. These are:

1. *Propriety criteria*. The rights of individuals are not abridged; the environment is not harmed; purposes should obviously not be unethical, callous, etc.
2. *Utility criteria*. There is an identifiable benefit to society; it should be responsive to some aspect of improving the human condition.
3. *Feasibility criteria*. The purpose is achievable in the real world, given the realities of such things as cost and political viability.
4. *Virtuousity criteria*. There is the prospect for fostering excellence, the development of knowledge, creative endeavor or advanced technical skill in an area of human endeavor.

These criteria are frequently conflicting and must be weighed and compromised in relationship to one another. For example, a historical review of industrial expansion from 1750 to 1950 would demonstrate that economic growth was feasible and of utility. However, propriety criteria regarding harming the environment were virtually ignored until relatively recently. In another vein, one could develop a school curriculum that meets virtuosity criteria but which does not meet feasibility or propriety criteria because it would cost too much and would ignore the needs of many students. These criteria can, like other tools, be used to help or harm people and must be used with good judgment and considered and reconsidered throughout a needs assessment.

The actual application of these criteria in assessing educational purposes to determine their defensibility is more a political than a scientific process. It necessitates contact with those groups that Guba and Lincoln (1982) refer to as *stake audiences*, that is, those who have an interest or involvement in the issues and programs in question. Such contact could take the form of meetings, presentations, debates, position papers, and so forth. The point is that in a pluralistic society different value perspectives should have the opportunity to be presented and considered even though this may be a difficult, if not volatile, process. And this process will probably lead to consideration not only of the defensibility of purposes but of their defensibility and importance relative to one another.

Clarifying purposes is a basic step toward identifying the things that are necessary and useful for improving or designing a program. Another important step is to reveal all purposes of the needs assessment sufficiently so that their legitimacy can be assessed. Many purposes are not defensible, given the tenets of a free society. For example, needs assessments could provide guidance for achieving such purposes as maintaining segregated schools, limiting academic freedom, discouraging women from seeking certain jobs, teaching contempt for the weak, removing the handicapped from the educational and societal mainstream, or developing a national hatred for people from another country. Whereas the assessments might effectively provide direction for achieving such purposes, they would be unacceptable, given the ideals of freedom and human rights. Likewise, a needs assessment could be done in such a way as to provide a rationale for a previously made decision. An administrator or board could decide to increase staff in order to employ a friend or relative and then conduct a needs assessment to justify that decision. A decision could be made to add or eliminate a politically popular or unpopular program, and then a needs assessment conducted to gather support for the previously made decision. Needs assessors must do all they can to insure that their services are aimed at the fulfillment of defensible purposes for both the relevant program and the needs assessment itself.

Purposes may also be evaluated in relationship to criteria that are derived from a philosophy. B.H. Bode (1933) described this approach as follows:

> When desires conflict, as they constantly do, a decision, to be intelligent, must be based, not on the quality or urgency of the desires, but on a long-range program.

It is the program, the more remote aim or purpose, that decides which desires are relevant and which are interlopers . . . the need is determined by the end to be achieved, by the underlying philosophy.

The supremacy of one philosophy over another, however, is debatable depending on how one defines such concepts as truth, good, bad, right, and wrong. Therefore, the defensibility of any purpose cannot be decided upon in a final sense. As might be expected, we encounter problems if we decide to review purposes from a narrow perspective, because the value or worth of a purpose changes with circumstances. Consider the following statement by Randall and Buchler (1960):

Authoritative and intuitive approval of certain kinds of ends and of certain specific ends neglects the fact: (a) that an end may cease to prove desirable in the process of achieving it; (b) that an end we choose cannot be separated from other ends we have chosen and will have to choose; and (c) that our ends may become undesirable in the light of circumstances external to ourselves

For instance, the aim of contributing money to an indigent person, though at first judged as good, may become bad in view of his extreme sensitiveness, or in view of the consideration that it may do us more harm than him good, or in view of the fact that a more urgent cause requires our aid, or in view of the discovery that the apparent indigence conceals psychopathic miserliness. Thus, for a critical morality the moral value of acts and goals can never be judged with finality in isolation but must always be examined in the light of possible consequences (p. 254).

The question of defensible purpose is seldom permanently resolved. We must continually assess and reassess our philosophies, purposes, and actions. This is a difficult and dynamic problem and not one to be ignored. It must, therefore, be a critical ongoing concern for the needs assessor.

Finally, we emphasize that defensible purpose in relationship to a program's goals is a political as well as a social and philosophical issue. There may be concerns about duplication of service, specification of responsibilities among personnel or agencies, and funding related to determining whether an identified need is in the service arena of a particular agency or program. A decision may affect an agency's budget and power, and such political factors cannot be ignored if a needs assessment is to be undertaken and completed successfully.

So what do we want the need assessor to do? (1) Help clarify the purpose; (2) examine it against criteria of defensibility; (3) clarify the trade-offs that are involved; (4) present a conceptual view of purpose and arguments for and against; (5) use the concept to search for needed things;

and (6) periodically review and revise the subsequent rationale and assumptions.

## The Needs Assessment Process

In light of the preceding comments, we propose that needs assessment be defined in general as *the process of determining the things that are necessary or useful for the fulfillment of a defensible purpose.*. In more procedural terms, needs assessment is the process of delineating, obtaining, and applying information to determine the things that are useful or necessary to serve a defensible purpose. Needs assessment can serve two primary functions. First, it assists in determining what needs exist and how these needs should be addressed. Second, it can provide criteria against which a program's merits can be evaluated, that is, the degree to which intended or important human needs are addressed effectively and efficiently (although in reality such use of needs assessment information is rarely observed).

The needs assessment process proposed in this book consists of five interrelated sets of activities:

1. Preparing to do a needs assessment
2. Gathering desired needs assessment information
3. Analyzing the needs assessment information
4. Reporting needs assessment information
5. Using and applying needs assessment information

These steps do not necessarily occur in a strict sequence since steps can be pursued simultaneously and because recycling will inevitably (and should) occur.

Preparation includes the activities that lay the groundwork for the collection and use of information. This is the delineation component of the definition of needs assessment presented in this chapter. It involves primarily two types of activities: planning and communicating. Planning involves the identification of the questions, design, participants, information collection procedures, analysis methods, and potential uses of the needs assessment information. Communications focuses on exchanging information with individuals, groups, and organizations and establishing workable relationships with the people who will be participating in or affected by the needs assessment. After completing the preparation phase, one should have an adequate answer for the following questions:

Who will address what questions?

With what methods?

Using what resources?

According to what schedule?

For what purposes?

The second step, information gathering, includes the development of both general and detailed plans of how information is to be acquired, the specification of procedures by which and sources from which it will be gathered, the actual collection of the information, and storage of the information.

Analyzing the needs assessment information, the third step, involves sorting, counting, and describing information; interpretation of findings; and the resulting identification of needs. This phase entails much more than statistical tabulation and calculations. For example, what if 32 percent of the elementary school population in a district fall below the national norm on a standardized reading test? Does this indicate a need? Additional information is required and should be carefully considered before this decision is reached. This information might include: the population's scores for at least the last three years: the literacy level of the parents and community; the nature of the student population (does it contain a relatively large number of bilingual children?); the students' actual functional capabilities; previous reading instruction, and so forth. This additional information would allow for a broad review of reading performance in the context of other information and would place the achievement test results in proper perspective, that of being one of several bits of information that could be used to assess reading needs. In short, a statistical finding regardless of its objectivity and empirical basis, does not equal a need. A need is a resulting decision coming out of a process that should include the compilation and review of several bits of information that culminates in a judgment of what constitutes need. It is this complex analysis and decision-making process that is addressed in the third phase of the needs assessment process.

The fourth phase of the needs assessment process is that of reporting the needs assessment information and results. The purpose of reporting is to provide a description of the needs assessment process and results that is accurate, timely, understandable, and useful to the relevant audiences. The needs assessor must have excellent communication skills and be able to write, speak, and display information clearly. An excellent needs assessment that is poorly communicated will probably have less impact than a mediocre one that is communicated well.

Using the needs assessment information is the last phase of the process and includes activities that depend in great part on the purposes of needs assessments. Needs assessments done for planning will involve the use of needs assessment information in a design or planning process. Information from a needs assessment collected as a part of a program evaluation may be used in a before-program/after-program analysis of the program's impact, to assess the value of the program's achievements, to determine if the original need is still present, and to identify new needs in the same area. How needs assessment information is used will vary with the purposes the needs assessment is to address.

The steps or phases of the needs assessment process described above are reflected in more detail in the following checklist. This checklist contains subpoints or particular objectives under each of the general headings and can be of assistance in planning, monitoring, implementing, or evaluating a needs assessment.

### A Checklist for Designing and Evaluating Needs Assessments

*Preparation*

- ☐ Identify and describe the client(s), other audiences, and target population.

- ☐ Clarify the purposes of the needs assessment:
  - ☐ Stated reasons
  - ☐ Unstated reasons
  - ☐ Defensibility

- ☐ Determine the scope and domain(s) of the needs assessment.

- ☐ Determine who will be involved in conducting the needs assessment.

- ☐ Develop and maintain the necessary political viability.
  - ☐ Involve key groups and individuals
  - ☐ Ongoing communication
  - ☐ Identify and adhere to appropriate protocol

☐ Identify and describe information needs:
  ☐ Setting
  ☐ Program variables
  ☐ Cost variables
  ☐ Philosophical and conceptual framework
  ☐ Outcome variables to be monitored

### Information Gathering

☐ Determine relevant sources of information.

☐ Determine sampling plan(s).

☐ Develop/select information collection procedures and instruments.

☐ Specify an implementation plan for each observation procedure.

☐ Specify verification and aggregation procedures.

☐ Implement verification and aggregation procedures.

☐ File and store the information.

### Needs Analysis

☐ Review and update all background information collected to date:
  ☐ Issues and concerns
  ☐ Changing conditions
  ☐ New developments

☐ Review the information base with the relevant groups.

☐ Conduct a descriptive (statistical) analysis as indicated by the type of information.

☐ Assess the available information:
  ☐ Technical adequacy
  ☐ Substantive adequacy
  ☐ Review analysis plan.

☐ Implement analysis plan:
  ☐ Specify type(s) of information to be analyzed.
  ☐ Specify purposes of analysis.
  ☐ Identify assumptions.

☐   Select and implement analysis techniques.

☐   Discuss the findings and formulate the conclusions.

### Reporting the Results of the Needs Assessment

☐   Review and evaluate reporting plan (see Evaluation Standards).

☐   Delineate the report(s) to be submitted:
    ☐   Audience
    ☐   Purpose
    ☐   Content
    ☐   Format
    ☐   Media

☐   Implement reporting procedures.

### Using the Needs Assessment Results

☐   Review needs assessment results.

☐   Articulate probable cause-effect relationships.

☐   Identify outcomes and objectives.

☐   Identify alternative strategies.

☐   Identify resources.

☐   Design a program in response to existing needs based on:
    ☐   Resources/apportionment
    ☐   Cause-effect relationship
    ☐   Feasibility

☐   Design an evaluation for the program.

### Evaluate the Needs Assessment

☐   Utility standards
    ☐   Audience identification
    ☐   Evaluator credibility
    ☐   Information scope and selection
    ☐   Valuational interpretation

☐ Report clarity
☐ Report dissemination
☐ Report timeliness
☐ Evaluation impact

☐ Feasibility standards
☐ Practical procedures
☐ Political viability
☐ Cost effectiveness

☐ Propriety standards
☐ Formal obligation
☐ Control of conflict of interest
☐ Full and frank disclosure
☐ Public's right to know
☐ Rights of human subjects
☐ Human interactions
☐ Balanced reporting
☐ Fiscal responsibility

☐ Accuracy standards
☐ Object identification
☐ Context analysis
☐ Described purposes and procedures
☐ Defensible information sources
☐ Valid measurement
☐ Reliable measurement
☐ Systematic data control
☐ Analysis of quantitative information
☐ Analysis of qualitative information
☐ Justified conclusions
☐ Objective reporting

## Summary

Needs assessment is a process that includes gathering and using information for making decisions about the direction or worth of a program or practice. Most needs assessments will address one or more of the following types of questions:

1. *Performance*. What educational outcomes are desired? What is the

desired and/or current performance of the people, program, service, etc. in question?

2. *Current or Potential Activities.* By what means can the desired performance be achieved, maintained, or improved? What are the overt and hidden long- and short-term costs associated with the current and/or potential activities (for example, money, time, space, morale, staff)?

3. *Decisions.* What actions (for example, allocation of resources, establishment of priorities, intervention) will be taken, given consideration of all relevant information?

Needs assessment is an ongoing, cyclical set of activities that is an integral part of the process of program development, implementation, and evaluation. It provides information about the good to be sought by a program and the characteristics of potentially effective programs or interventions. As a program is implemented or modified, a needs assessment can help guide decisions about the aspects of the program that should be changed and the directions those changes should take. The needs assessment findings, as the description of the needs to be addressed by a program, serves as one criterion against which to assess a program's worth.

The needs assessment process is not assumed to be strictly linear. The sequence of activities is not fixed and activities may be repeated. Additional information may be desired when the results of the analysis phase are reviewed. The approach presented in this book is generic and flexible. Details about specific activities of each phase are provided in the chapters that follow.

# 2 PREPARATION

The first task area in the needs assessment process proposed in chapter 1 is *preparation*. This task area includes planning the work to be done and involving key people in the needs assessment process. Careful planning of all aspects of the assessment is necessary, although not sufficient, to insure that the audiences are identified, that their information requirements are competently and efficiently served, and that they will make effective use of the findings. Key participants should be involved in the planning to provide valuable insights and to help prepare them to receive and act on the findings. Although initial planning is important, plans should be kept flexible and communication with the audience(s) should be sustained. The needs assessor must keep in mind the possibility that information requirements will change during the study. Needs assessment plans should be reviewed and discussed periodically to determine if changes are required to improve the quality and insure the utility of the results.

The main considerations in preparing for a needs assessment can be represented by seven general questions:

1. Who will be served?
2. How will they use the results?

3. What do they need to know?
4. Who will be responsible for conducting the assessment?
5. What procedures will be followed?
6. How will the assessment be managed?
7. What formal agreements will govern the assessment?

Questions one through four concern the participants in the assessment. The latter three address how the assessment will be done and lead to procedures for synthesizing the overall needs assessment plan, that is, a procedural design, a management plan, and a contract.

The above seven questions apply to most needs assessments—large or small. They might be handled quickly, as in a single planning conference between the needs assessor and the client, or they might require in-depth study and work by many people over an extended planning period. Even if the assessment is to be done quickly and with a small budget, the seven considerations should be addressed. Doing so essentially amounts to developing a defensible rationale and a practical plan for the study and insuring that plans will be reviewed periodically and modified as needed.

## Identifying the Client, Other Audiences, and the Target Population

An early step in the preparation process is identifying and defining the various types of people involved in the needs assessment process. There are basically three major categories to be considered: the client, the audience, and the target population. For purposes of clarity, the characteristics of each group are listed and explained below.

The *client* is the person or group commissioning the study. The client may be described by one or more of the following:

Financial sponsor of the study

Ultimate decision-making authority regarding the scope, content, and distribution of the needs assessment study

Person or group responsible for acting on the needs assessment report

The *audience* for the needs assessment includes all persons and groups who will be affected in some way by the study. An audience may be one or more of the following:

Program implementor

Program financer

Program developer

Governing body/policy determiner

Administrator

Supervisor/evaluator

It is important to identify clearly the client and audiences for two major reasons: to discover their different information needs and to increase the likelihood that they will be attentive to the results of the study.

Needs assessors can do a number of things to insure that the client and audience are correctly identified. An obvious initial step is to meet with the assumed client to clarify who the actual client is and what additional audiences should be served. Once the actual client has been identified, the needs assessors should exchange views about the needs assessment with the client, establish channels of communication with the client and other audiences, and reach initial agreements about the nature of the desired needs assessment. Subsequently, the needs assessors should meet with representatives of the other identified audiences, establish rapport with them, get their point of view about what needs to be done, get their general commitment to support and consider the study's results, and establish channels for ongoing communication. Throughout the needs assessment, it is a good idea for the needs assessors to maintain written records of their contacts with the client and audiences.

When identifying and communicating with clients and audiences, it is important to remember that not all key audiences are likely to be identified at the start of a study. Also, it is entirely possible that the relative importance of various audiences will change during the study. One way to remain sensitive to the issues of identifying new audiences and changing priorities among audiences is to have in mind a wide range of potential audiences. These might include concerned taxpayers, policy boards, legislators, institutional administrators, professional staff, professional reference groups, external sales and service groups, parents, and students. This list is simply illustrative and not intended to be exhaustive. Another means of defining and keeping in touch with a wide range of audiences is to establish a broadly representative advisory board for the assessment.

The *target population* refers to the people, program, or other phenomena about which information is to be collected and analyzed. The information collected may be on various levels in a given system. For example, in a school system, one may choose to collect information about individual students, classrooms, specified grade levels, a major division of the system—entire elementary or secondary levels or the entire system, grades K–12. The characteristics of a target population include some or all of the following:

Program participant

Program implementor

Program resource provider

Person responsible for the program environment

Program financial sponsor

Most needs assessments ultimately will focus on one or more *target groups* whose needs are to be served. These groups often, but not always, are students. Sometimes they are teachers, parents, or administrators. In other cases, they may consist of projects, programs, or institutions. In preparing to conduct a needs assessment, it is important to define the population of interest and to describe this population in relation to available information. Such definitional and descriptive preparation is especially important in regard to the designing, sampling, data collection, and analysis steps. In defining the population, the assessors should indicate who is included in the population and should indicate what boundaries separate this group from others. Such definitions are useful to *undergird* both sampling and measurement plans.

In analyzing the above categories, it becomes apparent that a member of any group may serve multiple roles. For example, a school board may be the primary client and also the primary audience of the needs assessment. In addition, the board may become a target population from which to gain information regarding current funding policies regarding a given program, the established methods of setting district and program priorities, and so forth. The main question that should guide this preparation step is, "Who is involved in the study and what is their role and function with regard to the needs assessment?"

In characterizing groups to be studied and groups about which decisions will be made later as a result of the assessment, the assessor should become knowledgeable about the current and projected number of units in both the study and projected treatment groups; the age, sex, and socioeconomic status of these groups; their location; relevant history, etc. The main objective is to bring together with clarity as much background information as possible concerning the persons, groups, programs, or institutions whose needs are to be assessed and served.

A variety of existing records might be tapped for describing the study population. These include building and district annual reports to state education departments; annual reports of relevant agencies, accreditation reports, community census records, evaluation reports, funding proposals, other needs assessments, students' cumulative records, and school census reports. By obtaining and checking such records, needs assessors can avoid needless duplication in their data collection and can form hypotheses about the characteristics of their study population which should then be checked further.

Considerable guidance in defining and characterizing populations may also be obtained by studying the underlying purposes and specific motivations for the study. In addition, it is wise to consider who or what might be treated as a result of the needs assessment. This suggestion raises a particular dilemma. It is that the group ultimately to be served, for example, kindergarten students in a particular school district five years from the present, sometimes may not be the group that will be studied. In such cases, the assessors should carefully formulate and present assumptions concerning how the study population may be similar to the future treatment population and should urge caution in generalizing from one group, time, or setting to another.

### The Purposes of the Needs Assessment

In the initial discussions about a needs assessment, the client group will almost certainly state why they want the study done. For example, they may say they want to know which students are most in need of particular services, which areas of the curriculum are most deficient, or what knowledge and skills will be useful to students after graduation. They may indicate a need to know such things in order to select students, initiate curriculum changes, choose objectives, report to the public, and/or allocate resources. The needs assessors should take concrete steps to identify the client's stated reasons for the study. Appropriate steps include interviewing the client and other audiences and reviewing pertinent background documents (such as minutes of meetings in which the needs assessment was discussed, newspaper accounts, and relevant correspondence).

While the needs assessors should strive to identify the stated reasons for the proposed assessment, they should also try to identify unstated reasons, since unstated reasons may be equally important as stated reasons and possibly of dubious ethical quality. Questionable unstated motivations for a needs assessment include justifying a previous private decision to cancel a program or to discharge an employee, enhancing the client's visibility and credibility undeservedly, or attacking an opponent's credibility. The needs assessor is unwise not to identify and consider such unstated motivations before proceeding. If there are unstated reasons that are legitimate but unidentified, the assessment may miss its mark. If there are unstated reasons that are indefensible, the assessors may unwittingly aid and abet an illegitimate use of the assessment.

Searching for and identifying unstated reasons for a needs assessment is a delicate task. Potential needs assessors should not avoid considering alternative perceptions about why the assessment is wanted, but they also must guard against creating an adversary relationship with their potential client when this is not warranted.

The recommended course of action is to inform the client that a decision to proceed will not be made until persons and groups who have reasons to be interested in the study have had an opportunity to give their impressions regarding doing a needs assessment and/or the direction it should take. In a forthright manner, the assessor should interview representatives of the relevant interest groups and ask the interviewees to identify relevant issues, documents, and other persons who should be contacted. After gathering information about the stated and unstated reasons for the assessment, the assessors should decide whether to proceed and should qualify and justify this decision in writing. The document in which this decision is discussed should be presented to the client and filed for future reference. The importance of this step cannot be overstressed since it insures that the decision to proceed with a needs assessment is documented and that such a decision can be defended or reviewed later, if necessary.

## Determining Information Needs

A plan for a needs assessment must be based on the ways that the client(s) and audience(s) will use the results. Therefore, needs assessors are advised to ask clients and other audiences to identify their interests and questions and the information that they would judge to be responsive to these questions. Structured exploratory meetings with the client and other audiences are one way to identify questions. The participants in these meetings should be asked to develop, review, and rank possible questions, recognizing that not all identified questions can be addressed. But it is good practice to first identify the broadest possible range of questions and then have the client and audiences rank them for importance and feasibility and thus narrow the focus of the study.

Once questions have been identified and ranked, the assessors should get the client and other audiences to indicate what information they hope to obtain from the assessment. For example, they should be asked to indicate whether they desire teacher judgments, students' test scores, in-depth case histories, or employers' judgments. They should also be asked to identify any existing records or other sources that they think would have this information. One way of engaging groups in a consideration of possibly useful information is to get them to develop or review outlines of possible final reports and sample tables that might be included in such reports. This approach will require them to think in very specific terms.

Items 1–4 below are intended to help the needs assessor consider a wide range of variables in identifying information needs and in preparing the data collection and analysis plan.

1. *What needs to be learned about the setting?* Collection and analysis of information concerning needs should certainly take into account the relevant context as an important variable to be considered in interpreting the findings. Often, it will be important to know the political climate, the economic conditions, the geographic situation, and whether this context is urban, suburban, or rural. By considering such variables in advance, it will be possible to arrange for the collection of pertinent data that are often relatively easy to obtain. Contextual variables, for example, are routinely reflected in daily newspapers; in minutes of board meetings; and in publicity information available from a chamber of commerce, a school district's public relations office, or real estate documents. In initial discussions with the client, it is advisable to consider what aspects of the relevant setting will be most important to describe and monitor during the needs assessment.

2. *What are the pertinent program variables of interest?* Quite often the primary variable of interest is a program. In other cases, when people such as students are the primary variable of interest, they are often involved in certain programs and it is the various aspects of a program that are of particular interest. Some examples are goals, procedures, budget, staff, facilities, impact, history, location, entrance criteria, etc. These variables can be considered and characterized through direct observation, program proposals, and progress reports. The needs assessor should carefully assess the extent to which such program

variables should be considered during the needs assessment.

3. *What outcome variables should be monitored during the needs assessment?* In many needs assessments the primary data of interest are the outcomes for individuals or groups in relation to the purposes of the program or institution in which they are involved. For example, the purpose of schooling, broadly conceived, is to foster, promote, and support the growth and development of students. Thus, a prime concern of the needs assessment may be to assess the extent to which the growth and development is as it ought to be. Such growth and development may be assessed and judged in the areas in which schools provide assistance. For example, outcome variables that might be monitored include achievements in intellectual, emotional, physical, aesthetic, vocational, social, and moral areas. The needs assessor is advised to help the client think broadly about the set of outcome variables that might be monitored in the needs assessment and then to select those variables that they consider most important. Although it is important to make some initial determination during the preparation phase, the needs assessor should also agree with the client that such determination will be reviewed during the course of the needs assessment and perhaps altered as more experience and information are gained.

4. *What information should be obtained about the cost(s) of the program about which the needs assessment is to be done?* There are always a variety of costs associated with any program, for example, developmental, maintenance, and opportunity costs. The needs assessor and client should consider what particular cost data should be gathered during the course of the needs assessment. Such cost data will prove useful later in helping with the assigning of priorities to potential needs and in the further analysis that must be done in determining what strategies should be pursued to respond to identified needs and what resources are required for implementing the strategies.

### Identifying the Agency or Person that Will Conduct the Assessment

The decision about what agent or agency will do the assessment should be carefully considered. Possible alternatives include personnel who belong to the organization in which the needs are to be identified and served, some external person or group, or some combination of these. Key qualifications include competence, perspective, availability, affordability, and credibility. If the person or group chosen to do the assessment is unqualified in any of these areas, then the success of the assessment is in jeopardy.

In general, some combination of internal and external agents is preferred. The internal personnel are often more affordable: they are already on the payroll and require neither extensive orientation nor significant travel support. If they are competent, available for the assignment, trusted by the client and audience, and, to some degree, independent from the program in which the assessment is to be done, then they probably should be assigned to do the major part of the work. However, it is still desirable to provide for an external audit of the assessment. Such a provision can lend quality assurance, technical support, an independent perspective, and credibility to the effort at minimal cost. Both the client and prospective assessor should proceed cautiously before deciding who should do the assessment. The client would be wise to consult with a potential assessor during much of the preparation stage without making a commitment about who will be commissioned to implement the plan. Likewise, potential assessors when contacted should make it clear that, while they are willing to advise on the planning of an assessment, they would be willing to implement the assessment only after assuring themselves and their client that they are fully qualified to do so and that the study is worthy of their involvement.

So far in this chapter, needs assessors have been advised to: (1) identify their clients, other audiences, and the target population; (2) ascertain and assess the underlying motivations for the study; (3) determine the general information requirements to be met; and (4) carefully decide what agent or agency will conduct the needs assessment. The point of the discussion has been that assessors should conduct a certain amount of preliminary investigation before agreeing to proceed with a study and before deciding upon the purposes and procedures to guide the assessment. Otherwise, the ensuing study may: (1) only reflect the predilections of the assessor or focus narrowly on the needs of one audience to the exclusion of others; (2) be done to serve purposes in the client's "hidden agenda" or not be sufficiently focused to serve important but unidentified purposes; or (3) provide information of only marginal utility. By conducting the recommended preliminary investigation, the assessor and client can be assisted in making informed decisions about whether and/or how to proceed with a study.

The following illustrates how the preceding advice might be applied in a typical school setting.

## Needs Assessment Planning: An Example

A superintendent in a district of 5,000 students asked the district's curriculum director to assist in planning a needs assessment for the purpose of identifying children with learning disabilities and assessing their particular educational needs. Furthermore, the superintendent indicated that the study should be completed by the end of the current school year and that about $5,000, in addition to a district staff member's salary, could be expended.

At first it seemed to the curriculum director that the superintendent was the sole client for the assessment. She had made the contact and had said she wanted to ascertain whether the needs of so-called learning-disabled students were verifiable and were being met adequately by the present educational system. She explained further that she could not count on the director of special education to conduct an objective assessment of this question because he was already persuaded that an expanded and expensive learning disabilities program was needed. For this reason, she had turned to the curriculum director to get help in finding a straightforward and objective answer to the troublesome question.

Further discussion revealed that the superintendent's request resulted from a directive from the board of education. This directive was given after the board heard a report from a group of parents who were critical of the district's lack of services for learning-disabled children. All of the parents reported having children of normal intelligence but with a history of poor school performance. They further reported that after much frustration in trying to discover their children's problems, they had obtained diagnostic services from a university-based achievement center for children in a nearby state. The diagnosticians from the center told them that their children fit the special category called "learning disabled" and that they needed specialized educational services. The spokesperson for the parents' group said that individually and collectively they had investigated the services the district provided in this area and had satisifed themselves that relevant services were almost nonexistent. They also said that in all likelihood there were many more parents and children in "our boat." They strongly urged the board and the superintendent to install an expanded, more effective program for learning-disabled children.

The board members thanked the parents for their report and recommendations and then discussed the matter. They quickly discovered that the district didn't have enough pertinent information to guide them to make an intelligent judgment about the extent of the problem. Therefore, they directed the superintendent to conduct a study to ascertain the incidence of learning-disabled children in the district and the adequacy of the present program for meeting their needs. After some discussion of this directive, it was agreed that the study should be completed by the end of the current school year and that $5,000 could be allocated for this purpose. Tentatively, it was agreed that the study could be conducted by staff internal to the district.

Having obtained this background information, the curriculum director realized that the client group included the board as well as the superintendent, that the parents' group and director of special education were key audiences for the proposed needs assessment, that there were probably other important audiences, and that the views of all of these groups should be taken into account. He related this perception to the superintendent, and they discussed the matter of client, other audiences, and target population. They agreed that a wide range of groups could be interested in the assessment and should be involved in planning the study. To provide an efficient means of involving the client group and various audiences in planning the assessment, the superintendent and curriculum director tentatively agreed to set up a ten-member advisory group that represented audiences in addition to the board. These included the staff of the special education department, classroom teachers, parents of learning-disabled children, school principals, and staff of the physical education department (which had been offering a Saturday class for learning disabled students). In addition, it was agreed that the board president, the district director of special education, and the superintendent would serve as ex-officio members. The curriculum director was to meet with this group as needed, but at least monthly.

At this point in the discussion, the curriculum director interjected that he might not be the best person to direct the assessment. He reasoned that some of the audiences, especially the parents who had introduced the concern in the first place, might not believe the results if they were obtained by persons internal to the system. The superintendent said she doubted that this would be a problem but agreed to withhold judgment until the audiences could be contacted about this and related matters.

Regardless of whether the assessment was to be conducted internally or externally, it was agreed that the advisory committee would serve a valuable function. Accordingly, the superintendent, curriculum department director, special education director, and board president met to draw up a slate of potential members for the advisory committee, along with a list of alternates should any of the initial invitations be declined. A letter of

Table 2-1.   An Agenda for the Initial Meeting of the Advisory Panel

| | |
|---|---|
| 1. Background of the problem | Superintendent and representative of the concerned parents |
| 2. Definition of learning disabilities, estimation of the number of learning disabled children in the district, report on what is known about their educational status, and a review of existing special education services | Director of special education |
| 3. Specifications for the desired needs assessment | Board president |
| 4. Financial, time, and personnel constraints | Superintendent |
| 5. Outline of the needs assessment process and identification of key issues | Director of the curriculum department |
| 6. Definitions of the client group, other audiences, and the target population | Group discussion |
| 7. Identification of key questions, associated information requirements, and desired reports | Group discussion |
| 8. Definition of the persons and groups responsible for conducting the assessment, including a discussion of the desirability of having the work done by an external group vs. one from inside the district | Superintendent and group discussion |
| 9. Next steps and planning for the next meeting | Superintendent and group discussion |
| 10. Summary and adjournment | Superintendent |

invitation over the signatures of the board president and superintendent was sent to the persons named on the first list. All but one accepted, and an appropriate alternate was recruited to fill this position.

The curriculum director—in consultation with the board president and superintendent—prepared an agenda for the initial meeting of the advisory panel; and the superintendent arranged for the meeting. The agenda is shown in table 2-1.

The results of the meeting are summarized in terms of the four questions addressed in the opening part of the chapter.

*Who Is to Be Involved?*

The *client* group was confirmed to consist of the board of education and the superintendent. *Other audiences* were listed as follows: the school principals, the counseling and guidance staff, the coaches and physical education staff, the school psychologists, the elementary school teachers, the kindergarten teachers, the middle school teachers, the high school teachers, the reading improvement and resource center teachers, the Parent-Teacher Association groups in each school, the staff of the special education department, and interested parents. It was recognized that the initial advisory group did not fully represent all of these perspectives, and the committee (including the ex-officio members) was expanded from 13 to 17 members. The resulting composition was as follows:

Board president (ex-officio)

Superintendent (ex-officio)

Director of special education (ex-officio)

Director of curriculum (ex-officio)

PTA president

Spokesperson from the concerned parents

School psychologist

Counselor

Physical education teacher

Elementary school principal

Middle school principal

High school principal

Elementary school teacher

Kindergarten teacher

Reading improvement teacher

High school English teacher

Middle school math teacher

In addition, it was agreed that group orientation and discussion sessions would be held with the presidents of the nine district PTA's, all of the school principals, all of the counselors, all members of the special education department, and all of the kindergarten and elementary school teachers (divided into three groups). Each member of the advisory group agreed to help conduct at least one of the seven meetings and that no fewer than three of the advisory group members would be present at each meeting.

At the first meeting the relative importance of the identified audiences was discussed, and, it was generally agreed that the highest priority audiences included the school board, superintendent, concerned parents, special education personnel, and elementary school principals. The rationale was that these groups would have more of a voice in making policy changes that might ensue from the study, while the other groups mainly would be involved in implementing new policies. Nevertheless, it was noted that all audiences had important perspectives and should be consulted in the planning of the study.

Defining the *target group* proved to be an elusive issue. The director of special education said that "in general, a learning-disabled child is one with normal or above-normal intelligence who manifests significant problems in learning that cannot be attributed to brain damage, vision, or hearing problems, or other well-known handicapping conditions." He further noted that the literature of special education is confusing on the matter of more precise definitions. He said that many such definitions exist, that they are very much in disagreement, and that there is no consensus about which definition is best. He said that due to a limited budget, his department had not been able to screen students to identify those with learning disabilities and that he and his colleagues have more than they can do just to keep up with referrals. Although there have been a number of children with classic symptoms of learning disability among those referred, he and his staff are unsure of the magnitude of the problem throughout the district.

He added that a special screening program—similar to those conducted in more affluent districts—might be conducted. However, he warned that the results of such a study, under the present funding structure for special education, would likely prove frustrating due to a lack of personnel and other resources that may be required to respond to the identified needs.

### What Purposes Are to Be Served?

After discussing the director's report, the advisory group emphatically urged that the district move ahead to identify the number of children with learning disabilities, to assess their needs, and to take whatever steps necessary to insure that the district provides the best possible service to these children. The director of special education asked how the necessary personnel and resources would be provided. The group responded that when the nature of the need becomes clarified, the district should consider a reallocation of existing resources and, if necessary, should pursue funding from external government agencies and foundations. Thus, the need for the needs assessment was reaffirmed.

It was agreed that the assessment should address the following purposes: (1) clarify what is meant by a learning-disabled child; (2) estimate the number of these children in the district; (3) diagnose the unique needs of these children by grade level; (4) characterize these children by grade level in terms of academic aptitude, school achievement, participation in extracurricular activities, and attitude toward school; (5) assess the adequacy of the district's practice in identifying such children; (6) assess the adequacy of the district's programs in relation to identified needs at elementary, middle, and high school levels; and (7) propose steps—along with general cost estimates—that the district might pursue to address the most critical of the identified needs.

The curriculum director swallowed hard in responding to these purposes. While he complimented the group for going to the heart of the matter, he also indicated that the scope of the purposes was ambitious. He suggested that the group move ahead to consider what information would be needed. But, he cautioned that the proposed budget of $5,000 might have to be expanded considerably or the scope of the study reduced.


### What Information Is Needed?

To help the group consider what information should be obtained, the curriculum director outlined the general purposes and procedures of needs assessment and then engaged them in a discussion of information requirements. He noted that, basically, the needs assessment should serve two purposes: first, defining the learning disability population; defining the critical variables of child development that should be supported by the district's programs: and identifying and analyzing both met and unmet needs for this group in terms of the relevant developmental variables. He characterized these as student-oriented needs.

He then defined the second purpose—addressing how to assist these children: "The task here," he said, "is to identify the school district programs and services that are necessary to promote the learning-disabled children's growth and development along the identified dimensions and to assess the district's present offerings in these service areas." These conditions he called program-oriented needs.

The director then outlined his view of the general process of needs assessment:

1. Reach an agreement on the definition of a learning-disabled child.
2. Operationalize and apply this definition to estimate the number of learning-disabled children in the district.
3. Define the areas of child development to be used in assessing the educational progress of learning-disabled children.
4. Identify possible information sources and select or construct appropriate instruments for assessing learning-disabled children in the designated developmental areas.
5. Identify the population (or at least a sample) of the district's learning-disabled children stratified by school levels (kindergarten, elementary, middle school, high school).
6. Collect additional information regarding the performance of the identified children such as test scores; grades; teacher, counselor, and parental judgments; and self-assessments.
7. Analyze the information to reveal variability and central tendency by "grade level" and to compare these results with school, district, and external norms.
8. Obtain judgments from various reference groups, including counselors, teachers, and principals, regarding the adequacy of the identified performance levels.
9. Collect and analyze judgments (especially from the advisory group) about the grade levels and dimensions of development that should receive highest priority if the present program is to be expanded.
10. Review relevant theory and research to identify the characteristics of programs judged effective in serving the needs of learning-disabled children.
11. Identify and investigate school districts with similar characteristics that are reputed to have done outstanding work in identifying and serving learning-disabled children.
12. Have the advisory panel define what they consider the most important characteristics of an effective learning disabilities program (such as screening, diagnosis, special classes, personnel, staff development, parent groups, resource center, budget, and philosophy).
13. Describe the home district's program in terms of the selected characteristics (see #12).

14. Collect and analyze judgments about the district's present offerings that are applicable to a learning disabilities program.
15. Collect and analyze data about the district's expenditures in areas that are especially relevant to the education of learning-disabled children.
16. Obtain information about funding programs outside the district that are interested in supporting the development of learning disabilities programs.
17. Collect and analyze opinions (especially from the advisory group) about which program areas should be developed, which strategies should be pursued, and what level of funding is needed.

Following this review of purposes and procedures, the advisory council attempted to list the questions and related information requirements that should guide the assessment. The results of this discussion appear in table 2-2.

Table 2-2. Questions and Related Information Requirements

| Question | Needed Information |
| --- | --- |
| 1. What is a learning-disabled child? | 1.1 A list of definitions and rationale from the literature |
| | 1.2 An assessment of the alternative definitions based on a critical analysis of the relevant literature |
| 2. How many children who fit the selected definition of a learning-disabled child are there in each school in the district and at each grade level? | 2.1 Review of instruments and procedures for identifying learning-disabled children at different school levels |
| | 2.2 Assessment, by school and grade levels, of 5% random samples of students to ascertain the incidence of "learning-disabled" and non–learning-disabled |
| 3. What is the educational status of the identified learning-disabled children in comparison with the identified non-learning-disabled and borderline learning-disabled children? | 3.1 Proposed variables and instruments for assessments in regard to intellectual, emotional, physical, social, aesthetic, vocational, and moral development |
| | 3.2 Averages and standard deviations of the three identified groups on the variables and instruments proposed in 3.1, summarized by school and grade level, as well as by group membership |

Table 2-2. (Continued)

| Question | Needed Information |
| --- | --- |
| | 3.3 Comparisons of the three identified groups by school and grade level on race, sex, and percent receiving Aid for Dependent Children assistance |
| | 3.4 Averages and standard deviations of grade point averages of the three identified groups, summarized by school and grade level, as well as group membership |
| | 3.5 Where feasible, comparisons of the performance data with state and national norms |
| | 3.6 Written interpretations of the obtained results for each school by a committee of the principal, three teachers, and (when available) a counselor |
| 4. What grade levels and dimensions of development should receive the highest priority if the program is to be expanded? | 4.1 Written proposal from the advisory committee about the grade levels and dimensions of development that should receive highest priority in an improvement project |
| | 4.2 Written reaction from the staff of the special education department to advisory committee's report (see 4.1) |
| 5. What are the characteristics of the programs judged effective in serving the needs of learning-disabled children? | 5.1 Written review of relevant theory and research regarding the characteristics of programs judged effective in serving the needs of learning-disabled children |
| | 5.2 List of school districts "like ours" that are judged by the special education department staff and the special education department personnel in the state department of education to have done outstanding work in identifying and serving learning-disabled children |
| | 5.3 Reports of visits to selected districts (see 5.2) by members of the advisory panel, including recommendations concerning the characteristics of effective programs for learning-disabled children |

5.4 Advisory panel report recommending the program characteristics that should be used in assessing the services their district provides to learning-disabled children

6. What are the strengths and weaknesses of the district's present program offerings vis-à-vis learning-disabled children and in relation to the program characteristics identified in 5.4?

6.1 Descriptions and judgments of present offerings by school and grade level and for the district as a whole by committees appointed from the faculty of each school

6.2 Independent assessments of the validity of the descriptions identified in 6.1

6.3 Cost analysis of the district's special education program

7. What external funding programs are potentially available to support a developmental program in the area of learning disabilities?

7.1 Collection of annual reports from foundations and an analysis to ascertain the involvement in funding special education programs

7.2 Results, similar to those sought in 7.1, of a telephone survey of potentially interested government agencies

7.3 Correspondence, regarding potential funding agencies, with districts with a history of success in getting state and federal funds to support their special education programs

8. What program areas should be developed, what objectives should be addressed, what developmental strategy should be pursued, and what level of funding should be sought?

8.1 Synthesis report from the advisory panel

8.2 Independent assessment of the synthesis report

As seen in the table, the advisory panel made considerable progress toward clarifying their information needs. On the other hand, it was apparent to all of them that more clarification and technical planning were needed. Realizing this need, they turned to the critical question of what persons or groups could be counted on to develop their rough needs assessment agenda into a feasible plan and then to implement it.

### Who Will Coordinate the Assessment, and How Should They Proceed?

The superintendent said that she thought the excellent leadership provided by the curriculum director during the meeting was ample evidence that he was qualified to manage the needs assessment. However, the director cautioned the group not to reach this conclusion too quickly. He said that his position within the district might cause some of the audiences to perceive him as biased and therefore incapable of conducting an objective assessment. During the ensuing discussion, the panelists said they recognized the problem being raised by the director, but, unanimously, they expressed their confidence in his ability to manage the study.

He thanked the group and said that he would be willing to proceed under three conditions: (1) that the group would be willing to help carry out the work; (2) that all should now agree that the scope of the study might have to be narrowed to fit within existing resource limitations; (3) that an external evaluator should be engaged to audit the needs assessment and thereby to enhance both the quality and the credibility of the study. All those present agreed to these conditions, and a decision was reached to move ahead under the leadership of the curriculum director.

We will leave the story here. This illustration has been given to show the careful thought and work that must be accorded to determining (1) the client, audiences, and target population, (2) the purposes of an assessment, (3) the information needs, and (4) the agent responsible for proceeding with the assessment. We turn our attention to three final questions to be addressed in preparing for a needs assessment.

1. What procedures will be followed?
2. How will the assessment be managed?
3. What formal agreements will govern the assessment?

**Developing the Basic Design**

Assuming that a decision to proceed with a needs assessment has been made, the assessors should then construct a basic conceptual and procedural design to guide the assessment. This design must reflect the decisions reached about (1) client, audience, and target population; (2) purpose; (3) information needs; and (4) assigned responsibilities for the assessment. It must also focus the investigation on the most important information needs and audiences, because often it will not be feasible to accomplish all that was projected in the preliminary investigation. It must provide a logical and practical guide to collecting, organizing, analyzing, and reporting the required information. And it should show how the assessment will meet and be assessed against the criteria of utility, feasibility, propriety, and accuracy (see chapter 6).

The primary audience for the design document includes all those who will help in implementing and auditing the assessment, including those who will govern, finance, manage, and/or evaluate the assessment, select samples, construct instruments, collect and file data, analyze results, and prepare and deliver reports. The members of these audiences invariably will differ in their needs for and abilities to understand the technical aspects of a needs assessment design. For this reason, the design should be organized to provide a generally understandable conceptual overview with more detailed sections containing the appropriate technical specifications.

An outline for a needs assessment design is provided in table 2-3. This outline divides the design into a *general design* for a broad audience, and *specification and technical plans* for task groups who will do the work. Each part is further divided into sections and subsections, and explanations and examples of the information to be included in each subsection are given. The divisions of this outline should be considered and used modularly, since often it will be necessary to submit a general design to some groups (for example, a policy board, a prospective funding agency), and detailed technical plans to other groups such as instrument developers, sampling specialists, and field observers. The outline serves not only as a guide for the various reports but can function as a valuable and flexible checklist to guide the development of both general and specific plans for conducting a needs assessment.

As can be seen in the outline, many decisions have to be made in the course of designing a needs assessment. These decisions should result from extensive communication with various groups as described in the preceding

Table 2-3.   Outline for a Needs Assessment Design

*The General Design*

I. Introduction

| | |
|---|---|
| A. Primary intent of document | For example, to provide a conceptual and procedural guide for identifying, ranking, and reporting on needs of a particular group in a certain program |
| B. Audience for the document | For example, the central study team, the board of education, the district administrators, the school staff who will collect data, the external consultants, and the external auditor |
| C. Basic definitions | For example, need, met needs, unmet needs, and needs assessment |
| D. Criteria for a sound needs assessment | Utility, feasibility, propriety, and accuracy |
| E. Limitations and caveats | Time and resource constraints that must be taken into account and special problems such as incomplete information about the purposes of the assessment |
| F. Overview of Document | Indication of which sections are most appropriate for each segment of the audience for the design |

II. Basic Information

| | |
|---|---|
| A. Background | Description of the events and discussions that led to the decision to do the assessment |
| B. Groups to be involved | Client, other audiences, target population, and needs assessment team |
| C. Substantive focus | Further description of the target population in terms of demographic variables, achievement levels, and special problems; and characterization of the relevant program(s) in which they are engaged |
| D. Information being sought | For example, more complete identification of the members of the target population, identification of their educational deficiencies, and strengths; location and assessment of services being provided to the target population; and identification of opportunities that might be used to serve them better |

Table 2-3   *(Continued)*

---

### The General Design *(cont'd)*

E. Uses to be made of the information

For example, to decide whether to maintain an existing program or to start a new one, to provide a supporting rationale for a request for external funds, to develop or modify program objectives, or to assess whether existing programs are effectively meeting the needs of those they are intended to serve

III. General Plan

A. Objectives

The specific intended outcomes of the assessment, such as: (1) to insure that the state board of education and other designated audiences become knowledge-able about the size, demographic characteristics, achievement levels, health status, and special problems of children of migrant workers in their state; (2) to identify the areas of a district's special education program that are not in compliance with given state regulations and to indicate what actions would be required to achieve full compliance; (3) to inform a school's principal about the extent that the school's teachers are aware of, skilled in using, and favorably inclined toward the resources and service for teaching reading that are available to the school; or (4) to inform kindergarten teachers in a district about the extent that their students on entering first grade evidence satisfactory levels of reading readiness

B. Logical structure

Specification of basic definitions: of a migrant child or reading readiness; description of a logical structure, such as a state's regulations for special education programs, a behavioristic theory of teaching and learning, a model of the change process, or a list of concerns and issues drawn from prior investigations)

*(continued next page)*

Table 2-3   *(Continued)*

### *The General Design (cont'd)*

| | |
|---|---|
| C.  General procedures | The main techniques to be employed, such as case study, survey of specified reference groups, and administrative hearing, testing, and content analysis of records |
| D.  Reports | Identification and brief descriptions of interim and final reports |
| E.  General schedule | An overall calendar indicating when the various data collection and reporting activities will occur and which groups will be involved at what times |
| F.  Evaluation of the needs assessment | Indication of how the needs assessment will be evaluated and how this evaluation will be used to guide the assessment and to help its audiences to judge its quality |

### *Specifications and Technical Plans*

IV.  Questions and Information Needs

| | |
|---|---|
| A.  Enumeration | A complete listing of the questions and items of information that will be obtained to address each one |
| B.  Comparison to objectives | For example, construct a matrix to show which questions and items of information respond to each of the objectives for the assessment |
| C.  Comparison to the logical structure | Explanation of how the selected questions and items of information relate to the logical structure to be used in guiding the assessment |

V.  Sampling Plan

| | |
|---|---|
| A.  Definition of populations | Identification of the basic groups about and from whom information will be obtained, such as first grade students in a school, a district's elementary school principals, or the children between 3 and 19 in the state who have hearing problems; indication of the distinguishing characteristics of each group; and general characterization of each group) |

Table 2-3  (*Continued*)

*Specifications and Technical Plans (cont'd)*

| | |
|---|---|
| B.  Sampling specifications | Specification for each population of the size and type of sample to be drawn and comments concerning the levels of confidence that can be placed in inferences from each sample to its population |
| C.  Procedures, timing, and responsibility | Specifications of how and when each sample will be drawn and who will draw it |
| D.  Special provisions | Indications of what will be done to secure as near to a complete response as possible and what will be done to identify any systematic bias in the sample that actually responded |

VI. Plan for Collecting
    Information

| | |
|---|---|
| A.  Instruments and procedures | Identification of each instrument and procedure, a description of its purpose in the assessment, an indication of how it will be applied and to what groups or set of documents, and examinations of its technical strengths and weaknesses |
| B.  Comparison to information needs | For example, a matrix showing which instruments and procedures respond to each question and information need in the assessment |
| C.  Procedures, timing, and responsibility for collecting information | Specifications of how and when each instrument or procedures is to be applied and who will be responsible for applying it |
| D.  Follow-up | Designation of procedures and responsibility for following up nonrespondents |

VII. Plan for Processing and
     Organizing the Information

| | |
|---|---|
| A.  Screening and correcting the data | Designation of procedures and responsibility for examining the basic information records and of rules for dealing with problems observed in the data, such as omissions, illegible responses, and randomly marked test answer sheets |

Table 2-3   (Continued)

---

### Specifications and Technical Plans (cont'd)

| | |
|---|---|
| B. Storing the obtained information | Designation of the system, procedures, and responsibility for filing and retrieving the obtained information |
| VIII. Plan for Analyzing the Obtained Information | |
| A. Analytic techniques | Designations—for each question and category of information to be used in addressing the questions—of the analytic techniques be employed, along with the rationale for choosing the technique and the means, e.g., the computer program, of applying the technique |
| B. Responsibility and schedule | Assignments of responsibility and designation of a schedule for carrying out the analyses |
| C. Comparison to information needs | General discussion of the adequacy of the projected analyses for addressing the specified questions |
| IX. Plan for Reporting the Results | |
| A. Formal reports | Fairly detailed outlines of each formal report |
| B. Provisions for informal reporting | General provisions and a schedule of meetings in which the progress and results of the assessment will be discussed with the different audiences |
| C. Responsibility and schedule | Assignments of responsibility and designation of a schedule for developing and delivering the reports |
| D. Comparison to information needs | General discussion of the adequacy of the projected reports for addressing the specified questions and serving the designated audiences |
| X. Plan for Evaluating the Assessment | |
| A. Criteria | Enumeration of the criteria to be used in evaluating the needs assessment |
| B. Procedures | Detailed procedural plan for evaluating the needs assessment |

Table 2-3    (*Continued*)

| | |
|---|---|
| C.  Reports | Identification and characterization of the interim and final reports of evaluations of the assessment, along with a designation of the audiences that will receive each report |
| D.  Responsibility and schedule | Assignment of responsibility and designation of a schedule for conducting and reporting the evaluation of the assessment |
| XI.  Appendix | Inclusion of instruments, job descriptions, vitae, report outlines, etc. |

parts of this chapter. Subsequently, the person(s) responsible for writing the design must engage in a complex conceptual and technical activity— transforming discussion and ideas into an organized design. The result of this process is a first draft design. Before being finalized, the design should be reviewed by the client and other audiences and, when feasible, by the person or group designated to evaluate the assessment. Any draft of the design must be considered as only the latest approximation. In many cases, information requirements change or become clarified during the course of the assessment, and various problems will be encountered. Therefore, needs assessors should plan to review their design periodically, and when problems are encountered to modify the design.

Design work conducted carefully and thoroughly can provide a basic guide for all those involved in the assessment and one which is accepted and understood by them. Moreover, it is an important determinant of the quality and impact of the assessment.

## Converting the Design into a Management Plan

The design discussed in the preceding section provides a crucial but not sufficient guide for conducting a needs assessment. A management plan is also needed.

The design and management plans often are reported and developed simultaneously in the same document. They are discussed separately in this chapter to highlight their unique contributions. The design indicates the overall approach to be taken to achieve the purpose of the needs assessment. However, the management plan is more detailed and relates tasks to resource and time considerations. Basically, the management plan should provide: (1) an integrated *schedule* of the work to be done: and (2) specifications of the financial, human, and material *resources* to be used in carrying out the assessment. Each of these aspects of a mangement plan will be discussed and illustrated.

### The Schedule

The sample outline for a design that was presented in table 2-3 included a general schedule and more specific schedules of sample selection, collection of information, analysis, reporting, and evaluation of the assessment. The scheduling section in the management plan is mainly an integration and further specification of the scheduling information drawn from the design. The schedule should show what tasks will be done by what groups during what time periods. A number of technical approaches to developing and maintaining schedules such as Program Evaluation and Review Technique (PERT) and the Critical Path Method are well specified in the literature. The Gantt chart technique is illustrated in figure 2-1. The chart has three dimensions: task, timing, and assigned responsibilities. A bar represents each task, with the left end of the bar indicating the projected starting date and the right end indicating the expected completion date. Initials attached to each bar denote the person or group to be responsible for the work.

Figure 2-1 is an example of a simple Gantt chart. In this example, the calendar along the top is divided into days. Depending on the scope and duration of the assessment, it may be more useful to divide it into weeks or months. The tasks are listed on the left side of the chart. Only a few sample tasks are included in the illustration. In most assessments, this list would be more extensive. It is useful to group these tasks into work packages that require team efforts, for example, sampling, collecting information, processing and organizing the information, analyzing, reporting, and evaluating the assessment.

The starting point and amount of time allocated to the completion of each task are denoted by the placement and length of the bar. For example, tests are to be ordered on September 1 and are expected to arrive by September 8. By looking at the arrangement of these bars, it is easy to see that some tasks (such as administration of tests) cannot be started until another task has been completed, in this case, delivery of the tests to the

Figure 2-1.  Sample Gantt Chart

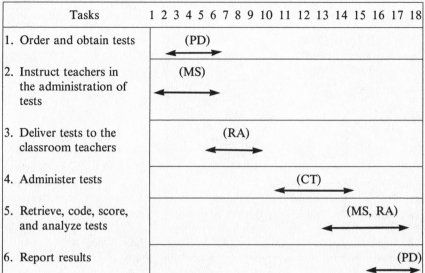

List of work groups: Project director (PD); measurement specialist (MS); classroom teachers (CT); research assistant (RA).


teachers. This type of chart also shows that some tasks can be done simultaneously, such as ordering and obtaining tests and instructing teachers in the procedures they should follow to administer the tests.

The groups responsible for carrying out the tasks are listed at the bottom of the chart. Their individual responsibilities are denoted by the placement of their initials by the tasks they are to accomplish.

The Gantt chart can be used to construct a staffing chart that shows more directly the work to be done during the course of the assessment by each group. This is illustrated in figure 2-2. Although figure 2-1 contains the same information, Figure 2-2 provides a more direct means of defining the work responsibilities of each work group.

Scheduling must be viewed as a process. Although it is important to construct, communicate, and use an initial schedule that reflects the design of the assessment, it may prove necessary or desirable to modify the design during the assessment. Therefore, the needs assessors should periodically

Figure 2-2.  Sample Staffing Chart

| September | Project Director | Measurement Specialists | Classroom Teachers | Research Assistants |
|---|---|---|---|---|
| 1 | 1. Order & | | | |
| 2 | obtain | | | |
| 3 | tests | | | |
| 4 | | 2. Instruct | | |
| 5 | | teachers | | |
| 6 | | in the | | |
| 7 | | adminis- | | |
| 8 | | tration of | | |
| 9 | | tests | | 3. Deliver |
| 10 | | | | tests to |
| 11 | | | | class- |
| 12 | | | | room |
| 13 | | | | teachers |
| 14 | | | 4. Administer | |
| 15 | | | tests | |
| 16 | | 5. Retrieve | | 5. Help re- |
| 17 | | code, | | trieve, |
| 18 | | score and | | code, |
| | | analyze | | score and |
| | | tests | | analyze |
| | 6. Report | | | tests |
| | results | | | |

review both the design and the schedule and, in consultation with the client and other participants, make changes as needed.

## Resource Planning

Effective implementation of the design and schedule depends on the provision of adequate financial, human, and material resources. These should be carefully planned and prespecified both to clarify what means will be available to implement the assessment and to define the constraints that should be considered in appraising the feasibility of the design and work schedule.

Again, it must be kept in mind that designing the assessment, scheduling the work, and designating the resources to be used are interactive activities. Moreover, they are parts of a planning, reviewing, and modification process that should be monitored throughout the assessment. Given these caveats, the elements of resource planning for a needs assessment will now be reviewed.

The basic elements of the management plan are the human, organizational, and material resources that will be required to carry out the assessment. Provisions in these areas should be prespecified as much as possible to give assurance that the assessment will be supported by adequate resources and to help establish the credibility of the proposed assessment.

**Personnel.** The *personnel* requirements of the assessment should be carefully determined by studying the design and schedule. Position descriptions should be incorporated in the management document. Often it is wise to append the vitae of the persons already recruited and to include letters that confirm their intention to participate. As a general rule, the planners of the assessment should recruit a team that collectively possesses the competence and credibility required to carry out the design and schedule of work. When the assessment must be conducted by persons who lack the needed skills, the staffing plan should include appropriate remedies, such as on-the-job training and assistance from technical consultants. Limitations in the credibility of the proposed staff—due, for example, to their lack of independence from what is being studied—may be offset by providing for the services of external auditors.

### Institutional Support

The needs for administrative arrangements, computer services, office space, and equipment should also be carefully considered. The likelihood that needed support in these areas will be available can be enhanced if planning and negotiation of these matters is done during the preparation stage. Delaying consideration of such matters until the implementation stage can result in troublesome delays, an inability to obtain some of the resources and services, and lowered staff morale—especially if they must begin their work before office space, furniture, and equipment are provided.

**Budget.** An obvious element of resource planning is a budget. It should meet five conditions: (1) It should validly represent the resources required to carry out the work. (2) It should be presented in a form acceptable to the financial offices of the involved institutions. (3) It should project expenditures for each fiscal year and permit the identification of costs for discrete work packages (such as preparing school level reports, preparing the district level report, conducting hearings, administering a community-wide survey, and undergoing an external audit). (4) It should specify costs for projected line item expenditures, such as salaries, services, and materials. (5) It should provide justifications for projected expenditures. Explicitness in proposed budgets will help insure that cuts in the budget, which often are necessary, are accompanied by corresponding reductions in the work scope. Procedures and formats designed to assist needs assessors in constructing budgets that meet these five conditions are discussed below.

The first building block for a sound budget is a list of tasks. This list should show the major work areas, the tasks associated with each area, the line item cost factors associated with each task, and the costs for each line item factor associated with a task by funding year. Also, the entries in this list should be coded numerically to facilitate grouping and analysis of costs.

Table 2-4 illustrates the budget for one task using this budgeting approach. It can be seen that the full cost of task 1.1 is $642; that this is its cost in the 1981 project year: and that it carries no cost in the 1982 project year. Moreover, the specific costs associated with this task can be given unique numeric codes by task, line item, and fiscal year, e.g., 1.1–103-81, which represents the clerical cost associated with the planning conference during the 1981 project year.

While the full specification of budget items to this level of detail is difficult and time-consuming, once completed, the resulting list can be enormously useful. It can be used to construct line item budget reports by year, to review the costs of major work areas, and to develop separate but complimentary budgetary requests when multiple funding sources are involved.

Two tables are provided to illustrate the aforementioned applications of the detailed cost analysis table in relation to a large-scale nationwide needs assessment. Table 2-5 is a sample line item budget by year. It shows the costs of each line item cost category and subcategory, by year. This table can be developed from the detailed cost analysis table merely by adding, by year, the costs for the specific items within each subcategory of each major line item. This type of analysis is particularly desired by grants offices and funding agencies.

Table 2-6 illustrates how the detailed cost analysis may be used to summarize costs by year and by work areas, such as sampling, collection of

Table 2-4.  Illustration of a Budget Planning Procedure

| Work Area | Tasks | Line Item Category | Specific Line Items | Cost 1981 | Cost 1982 |
|---|---|---|---|---|---|
| 1. Sample selection | 1.1 Conduct 2-day planning conference to define and characterize target population. | 100 Personnel | 101 Administration<br>2 staff × 2 days @ $50/day (planning × conducting conference and reporting results) | $200.00 | |
| | | | 103 Secretarial services<br>2 staff × 2 days @ $30/day (typing report, conference arrangements, preparing conference materials) | $ 60.00 | |
| | | | 104 Fringe benefits<br>20% of personnel costs | $ 52.00 | |
| | | 200 Contractual services | 201 Consultant<br>1 @ $100.00 | $100.00 | |
| | | | 202 Travel<br>Air fare $100.00<br>Lodging $55.00<br>Per diem $15.00 | $170.00 | |
| | | 300 General administration | 301 Telephone<br>20 calls @ $3.00 | $ 60.00 | |
| | | | | $642.00 | |

Table 2-5.  Illustration of Line Item Budget by Year

| Line Item | 1981 | 1982 | 1983 | Total |
|---|---|---|---|---|
| 100 Personnel | | | | |
| 101 Administrative salaries | $ 2,300.00 | $ 2,200.00 | $ 3,400.00 | $ 7,900.00 |
| 102 Professional salaries | 17,700.00 | 18,900.00 | 13,400.00 | 50,000.00 |
| 103 Secretarial | 6,675.00 | 7,725.00 | 5,200.00 | 19,600.00 |
| 104 Fringe benefits | 5,602.00 | 6,054.00 | 4,620.00 | 16,276.00 |
| 105 Travel, lodging | 1,690.00 | 5,590.00 | 1,890.00 | 9,170.00 |
| 200 Contractual services | | | | |
| 201 Consultants | 5,550.00 | 8,700.00 | | 14,250.00 |
| 202 Travel, lodging | 12,310.00 | 6,580.00 | 15,245.00 | 34,135.00 |
| 203 Computer programmer | | 1,500.00 | | 1,500.00 |
| 204 Computer services | | 5,000.00 | | 5,000.00 |
| 300 General administration | | | | |
| 301 Telephone | 360.00 | 360.00 | 120.00 | 840.00 |
| 302 Postage | 360.00 | 700.00 | 285.00 | 1,345.00 |
| 303 Printing | | | 10,000.00 | 10,000.00 |
| 304 Supplies | 1,205.00 | 1,460.00 | 1,810.00 | 4,475.00 |
| 305 Duplicating | 2,265.00 | 2,515.00 | 2,130.00 | 6,910.00 |
| 306 Miscellaneous | 200.00 | | 250.00 | 450.00 |
| Subtotal | $56,217.00 | $67,284.00 | $58,350.00 | $181,851.00 |
| 10% Indirect costs | 5,621.70 | 6,728.40 | 5,835.00 | 18,185.10 |
| TOTAL | $61,838.70 | $74,012.40 | $64,185.00 | $200,036.10 |

Table 2-6. Illustration of Work Package Budget by Year

| Work Package | 1981 | 1982 | 1983 | Total |
|---|---|---|---|---|
| 1. Sampling | $ 6,035.00 | $ 5,610.00 | $15,800.00 | $ 27,445.00 |
| 2. Testing | 20,805.00 | 11,850.00 | 27,040.00 | 59,695.00 |
| 3. Survey | 9,110.00 | 6,600.00 | 2,800.00 | 18,510.00 |
| 4. Evaluation of assessment | 3,000.00 | 1,950.00 | | 4,950.00 |
| 5. Analysis | 11,665.00 | 35,220.00 | 8,090.00 | 54,975.00 |
| 6. Reporting | 5,602.00 | 6,054.00 | 4,620.00 | 16,276.00 |
| Subtotal | $56,217.00 | $67.284.00 | $58,350.00 | $181,851.00 |
| 10% Indirect costs | 5,621.70 | 6,728.40 | 5,835.00 | 18,185.10 |
| Total | $61,838.70 | $74,012.40 | $64,185.00 | $200,036.10 |

information, etc. This type of analysis is of use to help funding agencies that may be willing to support part but not all of a needs assessment select the part they will fund. This type of budget breakout is also useful to the managers of large-scale assessments who need to allocate funds to the staff members of subcontractors who will be responsible for the various components of the assessment.

In general, budgeting is a crucial technical skill to be mastered and employed in designing and conducting needs assessments. This area is especially crucial in large-scale, complex studies, but small-scale assessments also need to be supported by an appropriate and easily understood financial plan.

## Reaching and Formalizing Agreements to Govern the Assessment

The final step to be discussed in preparation for a needs assessment is making a contract. This step involves clarifying the essential agreements that will guide and govern the assessment. These agreements attend to such issues as audiences to be served, questions to be addressed, information to be obtained, access of extant records, procedures to be followed, reports to be delivered, authority for editing and disseminating the reports, assistance to be provided by various groups, facilities to be used, schedule of work, and schedule of payments. Obviously, the agreements in regard to most of these issues should stem directly from the conceptual design and management plan, but some agreements, especially those pertaining to editing, dissemination, staff assignments, and financing, either will require further clarification or will not have been addressed at all. Reaching clear agreements about vital aspects of the assessment among the parties is in all of their interests, for the success of the assessment will depend on their concerted efforts, which in turn will depend on their collective understanding and agreements.

A key consideration in deciding whether a group should be involved in the contracting process is whether it will be expected to perform any role in the assessment. If so, the group must be consulted and its formal consent obtained. The importance of identifying  and negotiating with the appropriate groups cannot be overstressed because without their cooperation the assessment may fail and because they cannot be expected to fulfill agreements about which they were not consulted.

In general, the important areas on which agreements are needed are listed and described below:

1. *Identify the parties to the agreement.* An important initial consideration involves identifying the parties who must negotiate and agree to the assessment plan. Minimally, these include the assessors and the client; but, in some cases, the authority for the assessment should be distributed more broadly. For example, the authority group might include, in addition to the client and assessors, those who will finance and house the study and those will will provide data for it. The guiding principle is that those with responsibility for any aspect of the assessment should have authority that is commensurate with their responsibility, and they should have a voice in negotiating the agreements that cover their areas of authority and responsibility.

   The sequence of steps in deciding on the authority structure typically is initiated by the client group. They contact a potential assessor and discuss the needs for the study. The contacted assessor then, before agreeing to do the study, conducts some preliminary investigation as outlined previously in this chapter. During this process, the client and assessor should jointly identify and contact other potential authority figures. Representatives of all groups that would bear responsibility for the assessment should then discuss and negotiate the relevant areas of agreement.

   There is no one right way to determine authority figures for an assessment or to organize their policy-making and administrative efforts. However, in some cases—especially for large-scale assessments—an efficient procedure involves the establishment of a policy board and possibly one or more advisory groups. The main purpose is

to create an appropriate structure that will give those with responsibility for the assessment a voice in deciding how their work will be
done.

2. *Delineate each participant's responsibility and authority for carrying
   out or financing the various parts of the needs assessment.* This is
   especially important to settle at the outset of the needs assessment
   because various parties may later dispute such items as who was
   actually responsible for training teachers to collect the data, for
   collecting the data, for coding the data, for preparing it for computer
   processing, etc. Too often, needs assessors assume that they will get
   this kind of help from personnel in the client's institution and then find
   out that no cooperation beyond what was specified in the initial
   agreement will be provided.

3. *Specify the reports and other products that will be produced.* To the
   extent possible, those in authority should identify the main reports to
   be provided, give some idea of what will be included in these reports,
   and indicate when the reports will be delivered. In the process of
   deciding these things, needs assessors, clients, and the other authority
   figures often are led to revise their plans or expectations.

4. *Define the provisions governing access to the data.* Many times there
   are legitimate reasons for denying access to certain data to the needs
   assessor. In other cases, it would be legitimate for the needs assessor to
   have these data if agreements to that effect were reached beforehand. It
   is absolutely crucial that the needs assessors get these issues resolved
   before starting the assessment. Otherwise, they may become hand-
   cuffed by restrictions against their getting needed information because
   people in control of that information are unable to release it without
   some formal prior agreement or authorization. Provisions for access to
   data should cover both filed information and direct collecting of
   information from certain persons or groups.

5. *Specify who will have final editorial authority.* This matter certainly
   should not be left to be determined later in the study. It is crucial that
   the needs assessor and the client know where they stand with respect to
   final editorial authority. Leaving this unattended can lead to disputes
   or censorship.

6. *Specify who will have authority to release the final report (including
   the conditions under which it may be released).* In many cases, the
   needs assessor should insist on releasing the report to various
   audiences without any intervention or control by the client. This is
   certainly a reasonable step toward insuring the objectivity of the report
   and its credibility. In other cases, it may be appropriate that the client

be designated as the group to release the report but only after the needs assessor has approved the report for release. Also, it may be appropriate to specify that the report will include a main section signed by the needs assessor and a response to the findings signed by the client or another designated audience.

7. *Present the agreed-upon budget.* This budget should be completed in terms of all of the cost categories for the needs assessment, and it should be accompanied by a schedule of payments and specifications of accounting and billing procedures. This section of the contract serves to assure both the client and the needs assessor that the study is feasible in terms of the money to be expended and to insure that the money will be paid out in direct relationship to performance of the contract.

8. *Define procedures for reviewing and renegotiating the formal agreement.* Any contract should be subject to review and renegotiation. In most studies, unforeseen events cause changes in schedules and budgets. It is also possible that data once projected to be useful will become less useful if certain events occur or after other data are made known. Thus, there should be specific provision for the client and the needs assessor to review and make changes in the contract if unforeseen factors make it desirable to do so.

9. *Record the initial agreements.* Once the initial agreements, as outlined above, have been reached, the client and assessor should record and attest to them in writing. The written agreements may take the form of a formal contract or a letter of agreements. Such recording of the agreements will promote clarity and mutual understanding of the job to be done and the associated responsibilities. The recorded agreements will also provide a useful means of settling disputes along the way should they arise.

## The Example Revisited

Let us now return to the example presented earlier. As you will recall, when we left the example, the client, audience, and target population had been identified; an advisory council had specified the purposes of the needs assessment and outlined potential question and information needs; and the curriculum director had been selected to coordinate the needs assessment. The advisory panel had been very thorough in delineating the questions to be addressed in the needs assessment.

Table 2-7.  Tasks to Be Accomplished in the First and Second Years

| Year 1 Tasks | Year 2 Tasks |
|---|---|
| 1. Adopt district definition of learning disability and identify criteria of eligibility for services. | 1. Implement learning disability screening and diagnostic program and service. |
| 2. Develop screening and diagnostic program and conduct screening of 300 K–12 students to determine approximate incidence rate. | 2. Identify program and service needs of diagnosed learning-disabled students. |
| 3. Identify, observe, and compile descriptive catalogue of exemplary learning disability programs in the region. | 3. Collect and analyze judgments about what program areas should be developed; identify the development strategy to be pursued; and determine needed level of funding. |
| 4. Analyze records and current services for learning-disabled children presently being served and determine program needs and strengths. | 4. Collect and analyze data regarding district expenditures/budget/ potential financial resources. |
| 5. Investigate potential funding sources. | |

Given the short time frame for the study and the limited budget, the curriculum director immediately recognized the need to narrow the scope of the project for the current year. He busily spent the next two weeks preparing a list of tasks, needed personnel, schedules, cost estimates, and potential resources and then presented a summary of the material to the advisory committee. It was obvious that the time and budget were too limited to accomplish all of the tasks. The committee discussed the options available to them and finally reached a consensus that the needs assessment time frame should be expanded to two years and that the district should investigate the possibilty of obtaining external funding to supplement the district's budget for the project. Then the group delineated the tasks to be accomplished during the first and second years of the project (table 2-7).

The committee members recognized that an increased time frame meant additional commitment. The committee members were willing to commit themselves to a two-year project, however, provided a subcommittee on curriculum/programs was assigned to provide technical assistance to the advisory committee during the second year in identifying, ranking, and selecting program components to be implemented. The superintendent agreed with all recommendations and asked the curriculum director to investigate potential funding sources before submitting the recommendations to the board for approval. The curriculum director was able to identify two potential funding sources for the project. He presented a report to the school board summarizing the recommendations of the advisory committee and information relevant to potential financial resources. At the next board meeting, the recommended changes were approved contingent on the receipt of supplemental funding from one of the resource agencies.

In the following months, the advisory committee invested many hours in specifying the needs assessment design and management plan. The results of their efforts are summarized in the following documents which appear at the end of this chapter in Appendixes 2A–2E.

1. Gantt chart
2. Planning budget
3. Detailed budget
4. Memorandum of agreement
5. Grant award letter

These documents illustrate the range of decisions to be made in preparation for a needs assessment. They also show how these decisions can be recorded so that they can be studied by those persons and groups who must carry them out.

Several points about the example presented in this chapter are especially important. In the initial discussion stage, it is important to interact with representatives of a wide range of potentially interested audiences. These groups can shed light on the issues at hand and will, if involved early, be more likely to lend political support to the study team. Moreover, it is important to delay deciding whether to go ahead with the study until the need for it has been established and its feasibility has been confirmed. It is also important during this preparation stage to limit the scope of what will be done and avoid promising more than can be delivered. In general, the example shows that careful planning is important, even in relatively small-scale studies. Finally, documentation of the results of the planning, by preparing such items as a contract, a procedural plan, and a management plan, can prove invaluable for widespread communication about the study, guiding it, and possibly settling disputes about its conduct.

## Summary

This chapter has presented the idea that preparation is a crucial stage in conducting a needs assessment. Seven basic questions that should be answered in the course of planning and assessment were discussed: (1) Who will be served? (2) What purposes will be served? (3) What information will be obtained? (4) Who will do the assessment? (5) What approach will be followed? (6) How will the study be managed? (7) What formal agreements will govern its conduct?

Appropriate answers to these questions provide an essential foundation for the assessment. These answers are to be obtained through a preliminary investigation and negotiations among those persons and groups who will be responsible for the assessment. The answers may be refined and recorded in a design, a management plan, and a contract. Periodically during the assessment, such documents should be reviewed and updated.

The chapter contains suggestions on how the preparation might be done. It also includes an illustration to show how the preparation stage might be carried out by a school district with limited time and resources (see Appendix 2A–2E).

# APPENDIX 2A

## Appendix 2A
## Needs Assessment Planning Chart

| Tasks | Time |
|-------|------|
| | Weeks |
| | 1  2  3  4  5  6  7  8  9  10  11  12  13  14  15  16  17  18 |

1. Literature search

2. Summary report (review and compilation)

3. Review and critique of exemplary programs

4. Selection and approval by advisory council and school board of definition and eligibility criteria

5. Review instruments and procedures for identifying L.D. children at elementary and secondary levels and develop recommended screening program

6. Order instruments for screening eval.

7. Conduct screening program

8. Data analysis

9. Compilation and dissemination of report

10. Compile list of exemplary programs and review of program descriptions

11. Conduct on-site visitations of designated programs

12. Conduct analysis of programs and prepare program descriptions

13. Compile descriptive catalogue

14. Prepare description of current program and services

15. Analyze L.D. student records and observe classrooms

16. Analyze data to determine program strengths and needs

17. Compile summary report for advisory council

*Personnel*

| Project director | L.D. teachers | Psychologists | Classroom teachers | Consultants | Advisory committee | Spec. educ. director | Social worker | Diagnostic specialist | Secretary |
|---|---|---|---|---|---|---|---|---|---|
| PD | LD | PSY | CT | C | AC | SED | SW | DS | SEC'Y |
|  | ♦ |  |  |  |  |  |  |  |  |
|  | ♦ |  |  |  |  |  |  |  | ♦ |
|  |  | ♦ |  |  |  |  |  |  | ♦ |
| ♦ |  |  |  |  | ♦ | ♦ |  |  |  |
|  | ♦ | ♦ |  |  |  |  |  | ♦ |  |
| ♦ |  |  |  |  |  |  |  |  |  |
| ♦ | ♦ | ♦ |  |  |  |  |  | ♦ |  |
| ♦ |  |  |  | ♦ |  |  |  |  |  |
| ♦ |  |  |  |  |  |  |  |  | ♦ |
|  | ♦ | ♦ | ♦ |  |  |  | ♦ | ♦ |  |
|  | ♦ | ♦ | ♦ |  |  |  | ♦ | ♦ |  |
|  | ♦ | ♦ | ♦ |  |  |  | ♦ | ♦ |  |
| ♦ |  |  |  |  |  |  |  |  | ♦ |
|  |  |  |  |  |  | ♦ |  |  |  |
|  |  |  |  | ♦ |  |  |  |  |  |
|  |  |  |  | ♦ |  |  |  |  |  |
|  |  |  |  | ♦ |  |  |  |  |  |

# APPENDIX 2B

Appendix 2B
Planning Budget

| Work Area | Tasks | Line Item Category | Line Item | Cost |
|---|---|---|---|---|
| 1. Define L.D. and adopt criteria for eligibility for services | 1.1 Literature search | 200 Contractual Services | 204 Computerized searches 3 @ $60.00 | $180.00 |
| | 1.2 Summary report (review and compilation) | 100 Personnel | 102 (1) L.D. teacher @ $35.00 for 5 days | $175.00 |
| | | | 103 (1) Secretary— 4.5 hours @ $4.50 | $ 20.00 |
| | | | 104 Fringe benefits (20% of personnel costs) | $ 39.05 |
| | 1.3 Review and critique of exemplary programs—definitions, eligibility criteria, identification procedures, service delivery models | 100 Personnel | 102 (1) Psychologist @ $35.00 for 5 days | $175.00 |
| | | | 103 (1) Secretary—2 hours @ $4.50 | $ 9.00 |
| | | | 104 Fringe benefits (20% of personnel costs) | $ 36.80 |
| | | 200 Contractual Services | 201 (3) Experts @ $25.00 each | $ 75.00 |
| | | 300 General Administration | 301 Telephone—5 calls @ $3.00 each | $ 15.00 |
| | | | 302 Postage—20 @ 13¢ | $ 2.60 |
| | | | 304 Supplies | $ 15.00 |
| | | | 305 Duplicating | $ 10.00 |
| | | | 105 Travel | $ 25.00 |

| | | | |
|---|---|---|---|
| 1.4 Selection and approval by advisory council and school board of definition, and eligibility criteria | 100 Personnel | | |
| 2. Determine incidence rate of L.D. children | | | |
| 2.1 Review instruments and procedures for identifying L.D. children at elementary and secondary levels and develop recommended screening program | 100 Personnel | 102 3 Staff × 5 days @ $30.00/day (1 psychologist, 1 diagnostic specialist 1 L.D. teacher) | $450.00 |
| | | 103 1 Secretary – 7.5 hours @ $4.50/hour | $ 33.75 |
| | | 104 Fringe benefits (20% of personnel costs) | $106.75 |
| 2.2 Order instruments for screening evaluation | 400 Instructional improvement | 401 Testing Materials | |
| | | 5 @ $200.00 | $1,000.00 |
| | | 5 @ $35.00 | $175.00 |
| | | 5 @ $125.00 | $625.00 |
| | | Recording forms | |
| | | 2 Pkg. @ $3.50 | $ 7.00 |
| | | 3 Pkg. @ $4.00 | $ 12.00 |
| | | 2 Pkg. @ $5.00 | $ 10.00 |
| 2.3 Conduct screening program | 100 Personnel | 102 3 Psychologists @ $77.50 | Funding provided through current |
| | | 3 L.D. Teachers @ | district contract |

Appendix 2B
Planning Budget (Continued)

| Task | Subtask | Category | Item | Amount |
|---|---|---|---|---|
| | | | | $66.38 |
| | | | 3 diagnostic specialists @ $73.75 | |
| | | 300 General administration | 303 Printing summary forms | $150.00 |
| | | | 304 Supplies | $ 50.00 |
| | 2.4 Data analysis | 200 Contractual services | 203 Computer programmer | $125.00 |
| | | | 204 Computer services | $200.00 |
| | | | 201 Consultant—2 days @ $100.00 | $200.00 |
| | 2.5 Compilation and dissemination of report | 100 Personnel | 101 Administrative salary—3 days @ $125.00/day | Funding provided through current district contract |
| | | | 103 1 Secretary—7.5 hours @ $4.50/hour | $ 33.75 |
| 3. Develop descriptive catalogue of exemplary L.D. programs | 3.1 Compile list of exemplary programs and review of program descriptions | 100 Personnel | 102 1 Diagnostic specialist 1 Social worker 1 Psychologist 1 L.D. teacher 1 Classroom teacher 5 @ 5 days @ $35.00 per day | $875.00 |

| | | | | |
|---|---|---|---|---|
| 3.2 Conduct on-site visitations of designated programs | 100 Personnel | 104 | Fringe benefits | $175.00 |
| | | 102 | 1 substitute × 5 days @ $35.00/day | $175.00 |
| | 105 Travel | | 350 miles @ 23¢ | $ 80.50 |
| | | | 120 miles @ 23¢ | $ 17.60 |
| | | | 60 miles @ 23¢ | $ 13.80 |
| | | | 150 miles @ 23¢ | $ 34.50 |
| | | | 30 miles @ 23¢ | $ 6.90 |
| | 300 General administration | 301 | Telephone—20 calls @ $3.00/each | $ 60.00 |
| | | 302 | Postage—20 @ 15¢ | $ 3.00 |
| 3.3 Conduct analysis of programs and prepare program descriptions | 100 Personnel | 102 | 1 Diagnostic specialist 1 Social worker 1 Psychologist 1 L.D. teacher 1 Classroom teacher 5 × 2 days @ $35.00 | $350.00 |
| | | 104 | Fringe benefits | $ 76.75 |
| | | 103 | Secretary—7.5 hours @ $4.50/hour | $ 33.75 |
| 3.4 Compile descriptive catalogue | 100 Personnel | 103 | Secretary—7.5 hrs. × 5 @ $4.50/hour | $168.75 |

| Task | Category | Line item | Amount |
|---|---|---|---|
| 4. Compile description of current program and services | | | |
| 4.1 Prepare description of current programs and services specifying program, age levels, services, eligibility criteria, identification procedures, staff and number of children served | 300 General Administration | 104 Fringe benefits | $ 33.75 |
| | | 304 Supplies | $ 30.00 |
| | | 305 Duplicating | $ 35.00 |
| | 100 Personnel | 101 Administrative salary—5 days @ $125.00 | Funding provided through current district contract |
| | | 103 Secretarial—7.5 hours @ $4.50/hour | Funding provided through current district contract |
| 4.2 Analyze L.D. student records and observe classrooms | 200 Contractual Services | 201 2 Consultants @ $100.00/day × 3 days | $600.00 |
| | | 202 Travel—175 miles @ 23¢/mile | $ 40.25 |
| 4.3 Analyze data to determine program strengths and needs | 200 Contractual Services | 201 2 Consultants @ $100.00/day × 1 day | $200.00 |
| 4.4 Compile summary report for advisory council | 200 Contractual Services | 201 1 Consultant @ $100/day × 2½ days | $250.00 |
| | 100 Personnel | 103 Secretarial—5 hours @ $4.50/hour | Funding provided through current district contract |
| | 300 General Administration | 305 Duplicating—22 pages @ 3¢/page × 20 copies | $ 15.00 |

# APPENDIX 2C

Summary Budget

| Line Item | Local Education Agency | Ilston Foundation |
|---|---|---|
| 100 Personnel | | |
| 102 Professional Salaries | $1,325.00 | $ 525.00 |
| 103 Secretarial | 265.50 | 67.50 |
| 104 Fringe benefits | 346.35 | 118.50 |
| 105 Travel, Lodging | 188.30 | |
| 200 Contractual Service | | |
| 201 Consultants | 1,325.00 | |
| 202 Travel, Lodging | 40.25 | |
| 203 Computer Programmer | | 125.00 |
| 204 Computer Services | 180.00 | 200.00 |
| 300 General Administration | | |
| 301 Telephone | 75.00 | |
| 302 Postage | 5.60 | |
| 303 Printing | | 150.00 |
| 304 Supplies | 45.00 | 50.00 |
| 305 Duplicating | 60.00 | 10.00 |
| 400 Instructional Improvement | | |
| 401 Testing Materials | 914.50 | 914.50 |
| Total | $4,770.50 | $2,160.50 |

# APPENDIX 2D
# MEMORANDUM OF
# AGREEMENT BETWEEN THE
# SCHOOL BOARD AND
# LEARNING DISABILITIES
# ADVISORY COUNCIL

The School Board is commissioning a Learning Disabilities Advisory Council to conduct a study of the district's current policies and practices for serving learning-disabled students in grades K–12. The advisory council will conduct the study over a two-year period beginning October 30, 1980, and ending July 31, 1982.

### Members of the Advisory Council

The advisory council shall consist of the following representatives:

Board President (ex-officio)

Superintendent (ex-officio)

Director of special education (ex-officio)

Director of curriculum (Project Director)

PTA president

Spokesperson from the concerned parents

School psychologist

Counselor

Learning disability teacher

Elementary school principal

Middle school principal

High school principal

Elementary school teacher

Middle school teacher

High school teacher

Diagnostic specialist

High school English teacher

Middle school math teacher

## Questions to Be Addressed by the Council

1. What is a learning-disabled child?
2. What is the approximate incidence rate of learning-disabled students in grades K–12?
3. What is the current system for screening and diagnosing learning-disabled students?
4. What are the strengths and weaknesses of the current program in meeting the educational needs of the learning-disabled students?
5. What grade level and dimensions of development should receive the highest priority if the program is expanded?
6. What are the characteristics of programs judged effective in serving the needs of learning-disabled children?
7. What external funding program are potentially available to support a developmental program in the area of learning disabilities.?

## Resources to Support the Program

The school board has appropriated $5,000 to cover expenditures listed in the attached budget statement for the first year of the project. In addition, a grant has been secured from the Ilston Foundation of Educational Research in the amount of $2,160.50 to conduct a study of the incidence rate of learning-disabled students in the district. The School Board agrees to appropriate funding for the second year of the project not to exceed a total amount of $3,600. Final approval for the specific appropriation is subject to review of the proposed activities and budget statement to be submitted no later than March 1, 1981.

## Reports

The council will submit a preliminary report on July 1, 1980, presenting the major findings relative to questions 1, 2, 3, and 4, stated above in the section *"Questions to Be Addressed by the Council."* A final report summarizing findings relative to all questions is due on or before July 31, 1982. The council will be solely in charge of developing and editing its reports. It is understood that the council's report is to be as concise as possible and designed to communicate with the audiences designated for the report. The council has the right to disseminate its report to any members of the target audiences following completion of the final report and review by the school board. The school board may write and disseminate a separate statement to accompany the report.

## Target Audiences for the Study

School board

Superintendent

Concerned parents

Special education personnel

School principals

# APPENDIX 2E
# GRANT LETTER

Dear Superintendent:

The Ilston Foundation of Educational Research is pleased to inform you that your proposal regarding the Learning Disabilities Screening Program has been approved for funding. A total amount of $2,160.50 has been allocated for the projected. As previously negotiated, the following documents are due in this office July 31, 1980:

1. Detailed project description
2. Summary report of conclusions and recommendations
3. Project evaluation report
4. A copy of all instruments developed and a list of all commercial screening instruments utilized

I extend my personal best wishes for the success of your project. If you have any questions or if our staff can be of any assistance to you, please contact me.

Sincerely,

Harry S. Patterson
Executive Director

# 3 INFORMATION GATHERING

This chapter addressing the information-gathering activities in the needs assessment is presented in three sections: (1) Information gathering is defined; (2) the procedures for designing and operationalizing an adequate information collection plan are presented and discussed; and (3) the implementation of an information collection plan is briefly discussed.

## Definition

The information-gathering process, as it is defined and discussed in this chapter, includes deciding (1) how the "real world" will be observed, (2) how the observations will be made (interviews, questionnaires, etc.), and (3) how the resulting information will be recorded and analyzed. The term *observation* is used here quite broadly to subsume any investigative procedure that seeks to reflect or measure the way things are or seem to be, while at the same time recognizing that techniques differ in the degree to which they categorize and quantify phenomena and in other important characteristics.

Information gathering is not a simple, linear process evolving serially from deciding what to observe, observing, and then recording data from

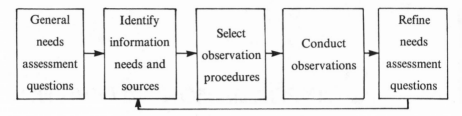

Figure 3-1.  Information-Gathering Process.

these observations. Rather, information gathering in needs assessment often proceeds incrementally from more general and open observation techniques to those that are more specific and narrow in focus. This process is depicted in figure 3-1.

In figure 3-1, the information-gathering process is designed and conducted in response to general needs assessment questions. Data resulting from these observations are used to further refine questions, which in turn determine the scope, nature, and specificity of additional observations. In general, the amount of recycling is determined by the initial broadness of the needs assessment questions and the specificity required for effective use of the results. A question with a limited scope such as "What are the mathematical instructional needs of a given group of disabled primary students?" will likely require fewer cycles of observation procedures than will a broad question like "What are the mathematical instructional needs of students in grades K–12?" The point here is that the process will vary with the level and type of questions to be addressed.

In general, information gathering involves collecting and recording information in response to the needs assessment questions identified in the preparation step. One of the basic assumptions of information gathering is that a need has no clearly defined existence. As defined previously, a need is relative and can be determined only as the result of a judgmental process that involves knowledge of conditions and factors pertaining to people and

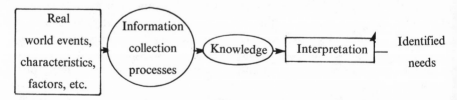

Figure 3-2.  Needs Identification Process.

organizations. This knowledge, when brought to bear against ideals, desires, hopes, and values, can result in judgments about the nature, magnitude, and significance of needs. The information-gathering step produces this knowledge for decision-makers who then interpret the results and identify needs. The general process is depicted in figure 3-2.

## Designing and Operationalizing the Information Collection Plan

The design of the information collection plan may be divided into five tasks:

1. Specifying the sources of information and the general procedures for obtaining the information
2. Determining appropriate samples of information sources
3. Selecting and developing the required instrumentation or procedures
4. Specifying a detailed plan for each observation procedure
5. Conducting observation procedures

Each of the above items will now be discussed.

### Sources of Information

Sources of information must be relevant and available for use. The relevance or irrelevance of any given source of information is not intrinsic but rather is determined by the relationship of the source to the needs assessment questions. For example, consider the following five potential information sources in relation to the question, "What settings are most appropriate for the instruction of hearing-impaired students?"

1. Pupils
2. Teachers
3. Special education experts
4. A sample of staffing reports recommending placements
5. Individualized educational programs (IEPs)

The sources of information most pertinent to this question are probably special education experts and teachers. However, if the question was "In what kinds of settings are hearing-impaired pupils in the district now receiving instruction?", IEPs would probably be a more appropriate source. For this question, the experts would be unlikely to be knowledgeable of current conditions. The most relevant sources of information are those that provide answers to needs assessment questions most directly.

When considering possible information sources, one should be creative in identifying diverse kinds of sources before selecting the source(s) to be used. Needs assessments often suffer from the expedient use of obvious information sources, such as the student achievement scores or teachers' perceptions, overlooking the less obvious sources that may be equally important. The broader the range considered, the more chance one has of selecting the best set of information sources. To assist in the consideration of sources, some major types of information sources are presented in the following list:

1. Products and work samples: lesson plans, IEPs, designs, diagnostic reports, etc.
2. Curriculum materials
3. Records and files: receipts, sign-out sheets, forms
4. Pupil data: test scores, achievement records
5. Literature: books, articles, journals, etc.

Since any given source is prone to some bias and error, it is also advisable to use more than one source of information to offset the distortion inherent in each. This sort of broad-based or triangular approach to using information sources is pictured in figure 3–3. If the needs assessment question were "To what extent are regular and special education teachers cooperating in planning instruction for handicapped children, a more complete answer could be obtained from all *three* sources listed below than from *one* of the sources: (1) regular education teachers; (2) special education teachers; (3) documentation in appropriate records (lesson plans, curricula); and (4) students. As mentioned previously, the information source must be both relevant and available, but it should also be one that can be used efficiently. A basic rule of thumb is to use sources that provide a reasonable balance among items of information.

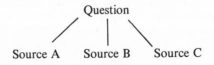

Figure 3-3.    Broad-Based Approach to Using Information Sources.

## Selecting Information-Gathering Procedures

Table 3-1 shows several methods that can be used in needs assessment. None of these methods is inherently better than the others. Rather, the methods must all be considered in relationship to use and desired outcome.

Selecting a measurement instrument procedure (the method of acquiring information from the source), like selecting the information source, is a relative matter. Procedures differ in many respects (for example, degree of objectivity, ease of scoring, cost), and the best procedure is one that will adequately address the needs assessment question at hand in light of several criteria, including:

1. Technical adequacy: reliability, validity, freedom from bias, inter-activity, etc.
2. Practicality: cost, political consequences, duration, personnel needs, etc.
3. Ethics: protection of human rights, privacy, legality, etc.

These and other factors that should affect the selection of information gathering procedures for a given needs assessment are depicted graphically in figure 3-4. It must be noted that one should consider all of these criteria, since disproportionate attention to any one may tend to violate another. It is usually necessary to reach a compromise that will produce a balance among these criteria without violating any of them to the point that the procedure is technically inadequate, unfeasible, or ethically indefensible.

Let us now consider the above factors in more detail in light of the needs assessment question, "What problems are teachers having when instructing handicapped children in regular education settings?", assuming we have decided that teachers are one source of information.

**Characteristics of the information source.** It is essential to consider the characteristics and background of the people providing information. How likely are the teachers to respond to various formats and procedures (for example, interviews, questionnaires, self-report/observation measures)? Is their educational and experiential background such that special termin-ology is required to avoid ambiguity or elicit complete and accurate information? Is a special incentive required to insure full participation? Will they be willing to provide the information required? What biases or particular problems of the group should be considered in designing the procedure?

Table 3-1. Information Collection Procedures*

| Procedure | What it Measures, Records | Example |
|---|---|---|
| Case studies | The experiences and characteristics of selected persons in a project or program | Several special education referrals are tracked throughout the relevant diagnostic sources to illustrate how parents are involved and react to these procedures |
| Interviews (group or individual) | Person's responses and views | Teachers interview pupils about school attitudes |
| Panels, hearings | Opinions, ideas | A panel of teachers reviews the needs assessment survey data to give interpretations |
| Records analysis | Records, files, receipts | Resource center files are analyzed to detect trends in materials used |
| Logs | Behavior and reactions are recorded narratively | Teachers maintain a log of disciplinary actions with pupils |
| Simulations | People's behaviors in simulated settings | Teachers are videotaped conducting a simulated diagnostic session |
| Sociograms | Preferences for friends, work, and social relationships | An IEP committee reviews their interactions during meetings |
| Systems analysis | Components and sub-components and their functional inter-dependencies are defined | The payroll and accounts payable processes in a school business office are depicted by a flow chart |
| Advisory, advocate teams | The ideas and view-points of selected persons | Teams are convened to debate the merit of two competing inservice plans |
| Judicial review | Opinions in the context of a systematic review of relevant information | A "jury" of teachers review the data collected on a pilot program to decide if it should be adopted throughout an entire district |
| Behavior observation checklist | Particular physical and verbal behaviors and actions | Record how frequently teachers use a new questioning technique |

Table 3-1.  (*Continued*)

| Procedure | What it Measures, Records | Example |
|---|---|---|
| Interaction analysis | Verbal behaviors and interactions | Observers code teacher-pupil interactions |
| Inventory checklist | Tangible objects are checked or counted | School bulletin boards are checked for inservice-related materials |
| Judgmental ratings | Respondent's ratings of quality, efforts, etc. | Experts rate the adequacy of the school's curriculum and schedule |
| Knowledge tests | Knowledge and cognitive skills | Faculty are tested on knowledge of state education laws |
| Opinion survey | Opinions and attitudes | Superintendents are asked to rate their attitudes toward collective bargaining |
| Performance tests and analysis | Job-related and specific task behaviors | Principals are observed and rated on how they conduct an interview |
| Delphi technique | Group consensus | Teachers inservice committee reaches consensus on program goals |
| Self-ratings | Respondents rate their own knowledge or abilities | Teachers rate how well they can administer different diagnostic devices |
| Survey questionnaire | Demographic characteristics, self-reported variables | Teachers report how frequently they use certain resource center materials |
| Time series analysis | Data on selected variables are compared at several time points | Frequencies of key pupil behaviors are charted over the course of a new reading program |
| Q sort | Self-reported attitudes | Administrators are asked to complete a Q-Sort regarding many aspects of educating handicapped students |

*Note: Sometimes these procedures can be "quantified," that is, categories can be established using numerical codes, so that numerical data are produced.

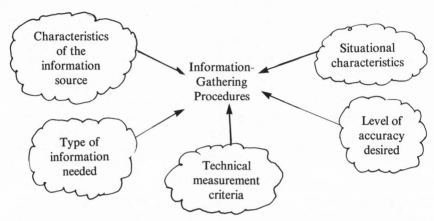

Figure 3-4.   Factors that Impinge on Information-Gathering Procedures

**Type of information.**   Information collection procedures differ based on the kinds of information they are designed to measure and record. If emotions, feelings, or teacher perceptions are of interest, then interviews, rating scales, and opinionnaires are applicable. In contrast, if level of knowledge or skill is required, achievement tests, analysis of work samples, or observations of teacher behaviors should be considered. In short, the particular kinds of information sought are a major determinant of the information collection procedure to be used.

**Technical measurement criteria.**   From the technical viewpoint, the needs assessor is challenged to design or select a procedure that is optimally valid, reliable, free of confounding bias, and least likely to interact with or change the information sought. Some procedures affect behavior that is under observation and require that steps be taken to minimize this effect. For example, the presence of an observer might suppress or elicit certain behaviors. Bias is present to some extent in all measures and should be minimized as much as possible. This can be accomplished with any given procedure through a variety of means, including training observers; avoiding use of negative, positive, or other leading statements in question- naires; designing sampling procedures representative of the population; and so forth.

**Accuracy of information.**   In cases where major decisions are to be based on the data collected, the data collection procedure will likely be designed more carefully than situations in which information is sought more exploratively (and will have less impact). In some cases, larger samples and correspondingly greater confidence in findings may be called for to permit finer discriminations or major decisions. If the district is considering whether to institute a massive inservice effort, then large samples and definitive information from many sources may be needed. Significantly less quantity and specificity of information might be required if the question is whether there is a need to include mainstreaming as a topic on a meeting agenda. The rule of thumb to follow here is to consider the possible costs and consequences of basing a decision on erroneous or insufficient data and to determine the degree of required accuracy accordingly.

**Situational characteristics.**   The setting and/or timing of an information-gathering procedure must be considered carefully. Would teachers' perceptions of problems be characteristically different at the beginning of the year as opposed to the end of the year? Legal, contractual, and policy constraints must also be considered—for example, would an unresolved teachers' bargaining agreement affect a survey or observation procedure and, if so, in what way? In summary, the design or selection of an information-gathering procedure should be based on consideration of the following factors: characteristics of the information source, type of information needed, technical criteria, level of desired accuracy, and situational characteristics. Careful consideration of these factors will increase the likelihood of obtaining information that will be accurate and useful.

### Planning Information Collection

Information gathering can be costly, and thus, economy must be considered in the sources and procedures. From the economy standpoint, the ideal information collection plan would tap just one source that would be so rich and accurate that it would adequately address all the questions of the needs assessment, as pictured in figure 3-5. Unfortunately, such an ideal

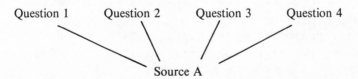

Figure 3-5.  Ideal Source for Information Collection.

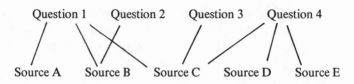

Figure 3-6.  Compromise Relationship Between Needs Assessment Questions and Information Sources

source is unlikely, and one must usually consider several sources and procedures. Economy and the need for multiple measurements may be conflicting concerns. A limited number of sources and procedures are generally less costly. However, the desire for complete answers and accurate information dictates the use of multiple measures which can increase cost. Thus, compromise is necessary.

This compromise relationship between the needs assessment questions and the information sources is depicted in figure 3-6. Note that each question, except 3, will be addressed by information from more than one source. Also, several sources serve multiple duty. Source C, for example, is used to address questions 1, 2, 3, and 4. Other sources such as A, address only one question and are thereby relatively less economical than a "bargain" procedure such as source C. A good information collection plan will arrive at this sort of compromise in which questions will be answered from multiple sources and the sources will serve multiple functions.

A useful device to facilitate this sort of planning is a simple matrix, which allows the planner to consider relationships among several needs assessment questions and several information collection procedures simultaneously. Such a matrix is pictured in (fig. 3-7) and displays the same relationship among needs assessment questions and observation procedures as in the figure 3-6. Note that question 1 is addressed by procedures A, B, and C and note that procedure C (our bargain procedure) will provide information for questions 1 through 4.

You will recall that the starting point of the information gathering process is the set of needs assessment questions identified in the preparation step. Likewise, development of a planning matrix begins with listing each of these questions across the top of the matrix (fig. 3-8).

The next step involves determining data collection procedures that could, considering the impinging factors discussed earlier, address these questions. This is done question-by-question, row-by-row, beginning with the first needs assessment question. Thus, for the example, we would identify a data

| Observation procedures | Needs Assessment Questions | | | |
|---|---|---|---|---|
| | 1 | 2 | 3 | 4 |
| A | X | | | |
| B | X | X | | |
| C | X | X | X | X |
| D | | | | X |
| E | | | | X |

Figure 3-7.   Observation Procedure Planning Matrix

collection procedure that could address the question "What are pupils' attitudes toward handicapped classmates?" As seen in figure 3-9, we might decide that a questionnaire to a sample of pupils could address this question. Reviewing the other needs assessment questions, we might determine that question 5 could also be appropriately addressed by procedure A (shown in fig. 3-10).

When all the questions that might be appropriately addressed by this first procedure have been identified, another data collection procedure is listed to address either the first or another needs assessment question and the process is repeated (fig. 3-10). Proceeding in this manner, the completed matrix for the five example questions is shown in figure 3-11.

The matrix is considered tentatively complete when at least one satisfactory data collection procedure has been assigned to each needs assessment question. At this point, it is wise to review the rough data collection plan with others to test its potential adequacy against the information needs of each client and audience and to review the estimated cost of the plan. Revisions to the plan can be made on the matrix by adding, deleting, or revising the questions and/or procedures. The primary test of adequacy is found in the answer to three basic questions.

1.   If we collected the information in the matrix, would we be willing to answer the questions and make decisions based on the data? (that is, are the procedures adequate?)
2.   Are the procedures cost-efficient?
3.   Are sufficient human and financial resources available to implement the plan?

A "no" answer signifies the need for revision of the planning matrix.

Needs Assessment Questions

| 1. What are pupils attitudes toward handicapped class-mates? | 2. What are the knowledge and skill deficits of handicapped pupils? | 3. What problems do teachers face in main-stream classrooms? | 4. What current services do handi-capped children receive? | 5. What problems do handicapped children encounter in main-streamed classrooms? |
|---|---|---|---|---|

Figure 3-8.  Building a Planning Matrix, Step 1: Listing Needs Assessment Questions.

Needs Assessment Questions

| Data Collection Procedure | 1. What are pupils' attitudes toward handicapped classmates? | 2. What are the achievement deficits of handicapped pupils? |
|---|---|---|
| A. Administer questionnaire to sample of pupils | X | |

Figure 3-9. Building a Planning Matrix, Step 2: Identifying a Data Collection Procedure.

The completed matrix represents a rough but comprehensive plan for the collection of information. As noted at the beginning of the chapter, the design entails five major tasks. Having specified the information sources and procedures on the matrix, four tasks remain:

Determining appropriate samples of information sources

Selecting or developing the instrumentation

Further specifying the logistics and operations of the procedures

Designing the data aggregation, verification, and reduction procedures

Needs Assessment Questions

| Data Collection Procedures | 1. What are pupils' attitudes toward handicapped classmates? | 2. What are the achievement deficits of handicapped pupils? | 3. What problems do teachers face in mainstreamed classrooms? | 4. What current services do handicapped children receive? | 5. What problems do handicapped children encounter in mainstreamed classrooms? |
|---|---|---|---|---|---|
| A. Administer questionnaire to sample of pupils | X | | | | X |
| B. Interview parents of handicapped pupils | X | X | | X | X |

Figure 3-10. Building a Planning Matrix, Step 3: Adding a Second Data Collection Procedure

Needs Assessment Questions

| Data Collection Procedures | 1. What are pupils' attitudes toward handicapped classmates? | 2. What are the achievement deficits of handicapped pupils? | 3. What problems do teachers face in mainstreamed classrooms? | 4. What current services do handicapped children receive? | 5. What problems do handicapped children encounter in mainstreamed classrooms? |
|---|---|---|---|---|---|
| A. Administer questionnaire to sample of pupils | X | | | | X |
| B. Interview parents of handicapped pupils | X | X | | X | X |
| C. Visit and observe a sample of mainstreamed classrooms | X | | X | | X |
| D. Analyze test scores of sample of handicapped pupils | | X | | | |
| E. Interview sample of teachers | X | X | X | X | X |
| F. Analyze records of pupil personnel services office | | X | | X | |

Figure 3-11.   Building a Planning Matrix, Step 4: Completed Process.

## Determining Appropriate Samples of Information Sources

Sampling is a shortcut. It allows us to save time and money by asking only a portion of all potential members of a population to provide information. Sampling increases the risk of basing decisions on inadequate information. If, for example, one needed to choose a hotel for a convention, a tour of all possible guest rooms would provide a more complete rating than would a tour of five rooms. But, the five-room tour is quicker, easier, and less costly.

The major purpose of sampling is to elicit an appropriate set of whatever it is that is to be recorded or observed. The observation procedure must be designed so as to insure that the sample(s) obtained are in fact representative of, or will provide a sufficient basis for, the phenomenon about which some inference or judgment is to be made. In a classroom observation procedure, for instance, we would need to consider carefully which teachers and type of teachers to observe to insure that those, who in fact will be observed, are representative of whatever it is we wish to learn about. In this case we would also have to be concerned about the sample of behaviors that will be available for observation. The presence of an observer, the timing of the observation, the setting, and other factors will all impinge on the behaviors that will be available for observation. A documents or records analysis presents similar sampling problems, but is not further complicated by dynamic observation variables.

In self-reporting or self-observation procedures, when the things observed or recorded are embodied in the respondent, sampling is equally crucial. The problem again is to insure that those who are selected to respond (or, in the case of voluntary response, those who *do* respond) are in fact representative of the characteristics about which we seek information. If, for example, information was sought about parent attitudes toward a new pupil busing scheme, a survey administered to PTA attendees could yield a biased view of attitudes since PTA participants may represent only a particularly interested or vocal subpopulation. Likewise, a relatively small return from a general mailed survey form may represent a biased subpopulation.

In instances when it is known that opinions, values, and so on will vary among certain groups or subpopulations, considerable demographic analysis may need to precede the sampling decisions. Knowledge of the nature and distribution of demographic characteristics can allow more efficient and appropriate sampling and lead to a better sampling design than one developed without considering demographics.

It is also necessary to consider the sources from which samples will be, or can be, drawn. It is entirely possible that the lists or other documents used to generate samples are themselves biased to represent certain subpopulations. The city social register, for instance, would not yield an appropriate sample of low-income respondents. A classic example of such sampling bias resulted in the famous major newspaper headline, "Landon Beats Roosevelt." The projection leading to this conclusion was based on responses to telephone calls. In 1932, most of those possessing phones were from the upper socioeconomic stratum, thus producing a substantial bias.

### Different Kinds of Sampling Methods

There are two general kinds of sampling methods: random and purposive (also called objective and subjective). Random methods are used to produce samples that are, to a given level of probable certainty, free of biasing forces. They allow use of inferential statistics to generalize findings with calculable degrees of certainty. Purposive methods are used to produce samples that will represent particular points of view or groups in the judgment of those selecting the sample.

Table 3-2 describes some commonly employed sampling methods, and gives brief examples of their use.

Table 3-2.   Some Sampling Techniques

| Method | How It Works | Example |
| --- | --- | --- |
| *Random*<br>Straight random sampling | One selects, via a random method (such as a random numbers table), a pre-determined portion of a population. The proportion of the population sampled determines the level of precision of the generalization to the larger population. The larger the sample, the more precise the generalization. | To assess reading levels in the district 5th grade, random samples of pupils are drawn to be administered a standardized achievement test. |

Table 3-2.   (*Continued*)

| *Method* | *How It Works* | *Example* |
|---|---|---|
| Quota sampling | The samples are drawn within certain population categories and can be made in proportion to the relative size of the category. A sample of parents, for example, could be drawn randomly from predetermined lists of upper income pupils, low-income pupils, Caucasians, Blacks, Hispanic parents, or whatever other subpopulation categories were of interest. The quota sample insures that the sample will include access to low-incidence subpopulations who would likely not be drawn in a straight random sample. | The university sends surveys to 5% of the graduates in each of several income and social categories to determine the perceived utility of the curriculum and its responsiveness to cultural differences. |
| Stratified samples | Samples are drawn from each of several "strata," such as freshman, sophomores, juniors, or seniors; or, teachers, administrators and directors. Stratified samples are useful when you have more, or a different, interest in one particular stratum than another. You identify strata of greater interest, then take larger samples from them. Each stratum is considered a population. | The school district sends an inservice attitude survey to all of 15 principals, 50% of 40 administrators, and 10% of 1500 teachers. |
| Matrix samples | This method samples both respondents from a defined population *and* items from an instrument. When the respondent pool is sufficiently large and there are many instrument items, it is more efficient to have each respondent respond to only a certain | To determine whether a district-wide workshop impacted on knowledge of new state laws, 10% of all attendees were given tests. To keep tests brief, each person answered only ten questions from the 50 |

Table 3-2. (Continued)

| Method | How It Works | Example |
| --- | --- | --- |
| | subset of the items. If these item subsets are randomly generated, and respondents randomly drawn, it is possible to generalize to the entire instrument. This method is particularly useful in broad-scale surveys or testing programs, but only, of course, when an individual's scores are not needed. | items on the entire test. |
| *Purposive*<br>Key informants | This method of sampling individuals is employed to access those persons with the most information about particular conditions or situations. Union representatives or de-facto leaders among teachers could be a prime source of teacher attitudes and opinions. Community leaders, respected individuals, etc., could yield rich information on community issues and so forth. | Workshop staff interview six participants to get their feedback. These six were selected because they emerged as small group leaders. |
| Expert judges | This method involves sampling those persons with exceptional expertise about certain conditions or factors of interest. When information about best practices or recent advances is sought, an hour interview with an expert in the area can shortcut many hours of literature review and reading. | The needs assessment staff conducted interviews with several teachers chosen by principals as being highly informed regarding mathematics education. |
| Extreme groups | This intentionally seeks out conflicting, or extreme, viewpoints. Whereas the random methods aim to account for bias and converge on the | Follow-up interviews are conducted with students who drop out of the program. |

Table 3-2.   (*Continued*)

| Method | How It Works | Example |
|--------|--------------|---------|
| | average or typical case, the extreme group sample purposely ignores the middle ground or common viewpoint to learn about the atypical, extreme view. The known detractors of a program, be they small in number and inordinately biased, can offer rich clues as to a program's potential flaws—and even strengths. | |
| Grapevine sampling | This entails a growing sample, in which each successive sample member is determined by clues, or explicit directions, from the prior members. One might ask a principal, for instance, to be directed to the most voluble, negative, positive, or reticent, etc., teacher in the school. That person would be interviewed then asked to recommend another person to the interviewer, and so forth, until the interviewer is satisfied that a wholistic view has been obtained. Direction to the next case can be asked for explicity, or derived from each case's notes. The same method can be used in a survey questionnaire, much the same as a chain-letter operates. | In evaluating a technical assistance system, the evaluator interviewed first the teachers who received service. Then, (s)he went to the person who advised the teacher to use the service, and also to the person who gave the service, using these contacts to get more contacts until repeats were encountered. |

Before we leave the topic of sampling, we should note once again that sampling is a shortcut and may yield inadequate information. In general, the larger the sample, the more sure one can be of the representativeness of the data collected, and generalizations will thus be more accurate. But, larger samples entail greater costs. Thus, the need for accuracy and completeness must be balanced against economic considerations. The reader interested in more information about sampling should consult the bibliography.

As with observation procedures, no one sampling method is inherently superior to any other, and they vary in terms of their rigor, complexity, cost, and so forth. The appropriateness of any given sampling method is determined by the extent to which it meets a given information need—again considering ethics, practicality, and technical adequacy criteria.

### Selecting or Developing Instrumentation

Up to this point, we have identified the information needs and sources relevant to the needs assessment questions. A crucial step is taken when this information is transformed into an instrument or other data collection procedure. Like other elements of the observation process, characteristics of the instrument or procedures are crucial to the integrity of the overall process and will affect the observation results. The most carefully constructed survey procedure and the most scientifically drawn sample will be rendered useless by an ill-constructed, confusing, or otherwise inadequate instrument. The term *instrument* is used in this context to refer to any recording form designed for a given observation procedure. This includes objective tests of achievement, the response recording form or sheet of notes for interviews, the recording or aggregation form used in record analysis, and other similar materials.

In data collection procedures, such as classroom observation and document analysis, that require a recorder other than the information provider, training in use of the recording form is necessary. Such training should provide instructions, experience in using the form, and deal with peculiarities or inadequacies inherent in the form or instrument. On self-report procedures such as questionnaires and tests, we rely only on the instrument to elicit and record the information. In self-administered instruments, therefore, we must identify potential problems and remedy them or account for ways in which the instrument may affect what is intended to be recorded. A knowledge test may, for example, contain clues and information that teach as well as measure. The phrasing, frequency, or juxtaposition of opinionnaire items may influence as well as record opinions. Confusing and ambiguous items or directions on a mail survey cannot only adversely affect responses, but make interpretation of responses difficult since analysts cannot be sure how respondents understood the items. Instrument format, length, readability, language and so forth, will affect the nature and frequency of response. Again, the remedy for these possible contaminating effects is the careful design or careful selection of instruments to be used. When possible, it is also wise to conduct empirical studies of instruments (pilot tests, field tests, panel reviews, etc.), making corrections and revisions prior to employing them.

Often, a needs assessment will tap existing recorded data and documents. In these cases, the instruments to be used will often be simple checklists, tally forms, and the like. While these recording forms must be thoughtfully designed, they will usually not impose major development problems and issues. Care must be taken, however, to insure that such forms contain adequate items and provisions for recording the desired information from the records and documents to which they will be applied.

At times, it is possible to use existing instruments available from libraries, resource centers, or commercial vendors. In these cases, the needs assessor must be a careful consumer and insure that the instrument selected will meet the projected information needs. The content, cost, reliability, validity claims, item format, response format, and purpose of the instrument must be considered carefully. A planning matrix, such as the previous example (figures 3-8 to 3-11) can be used to evaluate the instrument to insure that it is pertinent to each question it is intended to address.

Frequently, the particular instruments required for a given needs assessment effort cannot be found among currently available instruments, and it will be necessary to develop them. These homemade instruments will require further delineation of the needs assessment questions in order to develop sufficient items. As with commercial instruments, there must be careful consideration of content to insure that items are inclusive and responsive to the questions they are intended to address. Again, referring to the planning matrix can be useful in determining the content of the instrument.

Instrument development is a complex, technical task and may require assistance from specialists in the field. Drafts of proposed instruments should be reviewed and revised as many times as necessary and field-tested prior to their use. When data from a particular instrument are intended to guide major decisions or to undergo widespread public or expert scrutiny, increasingly greater investment in the development process may be necessary.

To serve as a guide in developing new instruments or assessing the adequacy of available instruments, instrument and item adequacy checklists (tables 3-3 and 3-4) are presented. While they are primarily applicable to questionnaire or multiple-choice types of formats, they can be helpful for other kinds of instruments. Again, readers desiring more information about instrumentation are referred to the chapter bibliography.

Table 3-3.    Adequacy Criteria Checklist for Data Collection Instruments

*Introduction*

( )    There is a clear statement of the instrument's purpose.

( )    The respondent is told how information resulting from the instrument will be used.

( )    Those who will see the data are identified.

( )    The respondent is told why s/he was selected to complete the instrument.

( )    The privacy of confidential information is insured.

( )    The anonymity of the respondent is guaranteed (if appropriate).

( )    Motivators for responding are supplied.

( )    Directions for returning the instrument are adequate (when, where, and how).

*Directions*

( )    Directions are given when necessary.

( )    The language used is apppropriate to the level of the respondents.

( )    The directions are clear and complete.

( )    An example item is provided (if necessary).

( )    Directions are provided for responding to items which "do not apply."

( )    The respondent is told if other materials are needed to complete to complete the instrument.

*Format*

( )    Individual items are appropriately spaced.

( )    Items are grouped in a logical order (by content, type, etc.).

( )    Sufficient space exists for the desired response.

( )    Instrument is easy to read.

( )    Instrument is not too long.

( )    Instrument is "pleasing to the eye."

Table 3-4. Adequacy Criteria for Instrument Items

| *Item Stems* | *Responses* |
|---|---|
| Item stems are relevant to the instrument's purpose; each measures a single dimension; language is clear, complete, understandable; bias is not introduced; the unit of response is specified; and, when appropriate, items are independent of one another. | Response categories are relevant to stems, measure only one dimension, do not encourage misrepresentation or distortion in reporting events, and, when appropriate, provide guidelines for open-ended responses/comments. |

( ) The stem is relevant to the stated purpose of the instrument.
( ) The stem is unidimensional.
( ) The wording of the stem is appropriate to the reading level of the respondents.
( ) The possible response is not biased by the wording of the stem.
( ) "Supply" items identify the appropriate unit of response.
( ) Each stem is independent of other stems.
( ) The level of analysis necessary to respond to the stem is appropriate to the capabilities of the respondents.

( ) Response categories are unidimensional.
( ) Response categories are non-overlapping.
( ) Response categories are exhaustive (if appropriate).
( ) Response categories are relevant to the stems.
( ) "Not applicable" options are provided where appropriate.
( ) "I don't know" options are provided where appropriate.
( ) "No opinion" options are provided where appropriate.
( ) A sufficient amount of space is left for supply responses.
( ) Space is provided for comments where appropriate.
( ) Guidelines are provided for comments (if appropriate).

## Further Specifying the Plan for the Observation Procedure

Basically, this step calls for the preparation and decisions required to get to the point of being able to say, for any given observation procedure: "Ready! Now let's go collect the information."

Several considerations and decisions must be addressed:

1. Who will conduct the observations, measurements, etc.
2. When observations are to be made, instruments administered, etc.

3. Where the observations or instruments are to be administered
4. Pertinent schedules for respondents or observers to follow
5. How instruments or recording forms are to be returned, to whom, and when
6. Other administrative or logistic details as appropriate

In observation procedures where the observer is external to the object of observation (as in behavioral observation, checklists, site visits, a document analysis, and so forth), the persons conducting the measurements are crucial elements in the process. The major consideration for this element is whether the observer or recorder can accurately make the judgments, classifications, and responses required for the optimal operation of the procedure, or whether peculiarities of the observer/recorder will adversely affect the data collected. In the case of a behavioral observation, site visits, document analyses, etc., it may be necessary to train people how to implement the observation procedure. Likewise, when several observers or raters will be employed, training is necessary to insure consistent ratings of the phenomena by the observers (i.e., interrater reliability).

Observation procedures, occurring as they do at particular points in time and space are necessarily situation-specfific. They must therefore be designed to minimize the extent to which characteristics peculiar to the *process* of observation may bias or otherwise adversely affect the data collected. The time, place, and context of observation can and will affect the data, as will the attitudes, motivation, and other characteristics of the respondent. Opinion surveys are notoriously susceptible to environmental factors (current events, etc.), and thus in both the planning of the survey and interpretation of its data, one will want to consider these factors. How, when, and by whom an interview is conducted can affect responses as much as or even more than the views of the respondent. A tester or observer's directions and demeanor, the time of day, the room in which a test or observation takes place, can introduce variance into the most objective test and affect the behavior observed. Almost any process or situational factor can affect an observation process. The trick in good data collection is to consider as many of these potential factors as possible and account for their interaction in the design, implementation, and interpretation of observation procedures.

With these factors in mind, a plan for conducting each observation procedure should be detailed. This plan should provide details pertinent to each of the items listed above (who, when, where, etc.).

## Conducting Observation Procedures

A good data collection design can set the stage for gathering useful information, but the implementation of the design is the crucial step. Needs assessors must make adequate preparation to implement their data collection plans appropriately, and safely and adequately store and file data so that they will be available when needed. The following areas of concern or activity are basic to the successful implementation of the information gathering plan.

**Follow appropriate protocol; obtain necessary clearances, permission, and releases.**   In many cases, some information and data will simply not be available unless certain permissions and releases are obtained. Some files, records, and persons are not routinely accessible without prior arrangements. In other cases, failure to allow appropriate protocol may affect the samples or nature of data obtained. An interviewer, for instance, may receive a frosty "welcome" and little more if appropriate protocol and arrangements have not been followed. Data obtained without appropriate releases or permissions may be unuseable, or even result in legal complaints. Care must be taken to respect an individual's rights, prerequisites and authorities and to adhere to legal and ethical guidelines.

**Adhere to good measure practices.**   Earlier in this chapter, we discussed the extent to which situational factors can influence data collection. It is important to adhere to the proper procedures for the respective data collection procedure, so that situational characteristics will not adversely affect the data. All aspects of the distribution, administration, and return of instruments should be consistent in all instances. If pupils in one school, for instance, did not receive the same test instructions that others did, their scores will likely be biased. Similarly, a survey distributed by mail in one district, yet carried home by pupils in another, may yield substantively different response samples and perhaps biased results. An interviewer who clarifies, repeats, and rephrases questions will gather different responses than an interviewer who does not. In all of these cases, inconsistencies and differences in the data collection procedures can influence their results. Procedures must therefore be designed so they will inhibit such inconsistencies and be monitored and reviewed to detect confounding factors when they occur.

A cautionary note is in order here. Care must likewise be taken not to allow rigid adherence to an observation design to adversely affect the data collection when it is obvious from existing conditions that revisions and adjustments must be made. If, for instance, an interviewer has traveled 50 miles to meet with a superintendent, but finds that some circumstance prohibits the superintendent's participation, it would probably be unwise to reject the offer to interview the assistant superintendent. The best laid plans are bound to need revision in the face of current events. Such revisions ought to be made when needed, with care taken to document them when they occur so that their potential consequences to the data collected can be considered.

**Aggregation and verification.** In many instances, data resulting from needs assessment efforts will require reduction and aggregation before they can be analyzed. In general, the larger the scope of information collection and the greater the number of completed instruments or forms, the more complex the aggregation and reduction scheme will have to be. On the other hand, it is critical to bear in mind that aggregation and reduction of *any* sort, while it can aid communication and interpretation, can remove meaning. For this reason, the less reduction, the better. The closer data are to their original, raw form, the richer they will be. A brief review of a dozen one-page workshop feedback forms may be more informative than the same amount of time spent reviewing a one-page presentation of descriptive statistics derived from these forms.

With the example of a large-scale questionnaire survey, for instance, careful planning is required to insure that each form is returned and pertinent data gleaned from it and prepared for analysis. Coding forms or other devices to record and portray each instrument's data need to be designed. The task of transferring data from completed instruments to a coding form is a simple clerical task but one which, if ill-planned or carried out lackadaisically, can ruin the entire data collection effort. The aggregation and recording system must be accurate so that the data are not changed by the aggregation process. The system must also be comprehensive, insuring that all instrument items are recorded. In addition, extra information, such as date of receipt or other pertinent variables may be included on the coding form. Finally, the aggregation system should be simple. Unnecessary complexity is likely to introduce error and contaminate the data needlessly.

Once aggregated or otherwise recorded, returned data should be verified, or "cleaned." In essence, this step recognizes the practical notion that some data may not be worth the trouble and expense of analysis. Some questionnaires may be only partially complete: records analyses might include data from clearly incomplete or inaccurate records; interviews may be incomplete; test items and questionnaires may not have been taken seriously. All of these phenomena may produce data that are clearly untrustworthy and ought to be rejected from a sample and not included for analysis.

Rules for determining just which data bits or returned instruments will be included for analysis are necessary. A survey analysis scheme may determine, for instance, that any instrument with less than 75 percent completion will be rejected from the sample. Or we may decide not to further analyze any interview data resulting from a session that lasted less than ten minutes. Such rules are necessarily arbitrary and probably cannot be made until we have a notion of how the data actually look. In any case, however, there must be a defensible rationale for any such rules, and their possible biasing or contaminating consequences ought to be considered.

**Filing and storing data.** This aspect of the observation procedures step has a dual function. The data collector must make information readily available in an interpretable form to those who must judge needs, and the data collector must honor the vested public and individual trusts for and about whom these data were collected. For all data collected, a record should be maintained of each aggregation or reduction step, with the source data appropriately referenced and stored so that it might be retrieved to verify or reanalyze it as may be necessary. Thus, the original set of survey forms should not be destroyed as soon as a frequency analysis is completed, for it may be useful at a later date to return to these raw data for verification or a new analysis. When computer facilities are used, of course, data tapes and disks can greatly ease the storage burden. Reports and interim analyses or aggregations should also be referenced, stored, or filed so they can easily be accessed when needed.

Care must be taken to insure that data and all reports based on them are responsibly handled, distributed, and stored. Irresponsible or otherwise, inadequate handling can do great harm to people and their rights. Even without legal or ethical infringements, irresponsibility in the handling of needs assessment data can do grave harm to future data collection efforts. We all live in a world of decreasing privacy and should do all we can to be attentive to people's rights and feelings.

# 4 ANALYSIS

This chapter focuses on the process and procedures involved in analyzing information. For purposes of explanation and illustration, analysis is presented in this chapter as an independent stage in the needs assessment process. In reality, analysis is intertwined with the other needs assessment activities—preparation, collection of information, and reporting—and must be considered throughout the entire needs assessment process.

Analysis is not simply a mechanical process of choosing and applying statistical procedures but involves specification and justification of assumptions, rules, and procedures for interpretation of information. The process of analysis involves efforts that are thoughtful, investigatory, systematic, and carefully recorded so that they can be replicated and reviewed. The primary goal of analysis is to bring meaning to the obtained information and to do so in the context of some philosophy, relevant perspectives, and value positions that may be in conflict. Although analyses should be well organized and reproducible, the reader must recognize that all analyses necessarily are based on decisions that are subjective, as, for example, the choice of performance criteria. There is no objective reality or unassailable philosophy that can serve as the final authority for analysis plans. Rather, people acting as responsibly and rationally as they can must use their best judgment and all their wits in investigating and interpreting the obtained information. This is the essence of the analysis process.

Analysis must also be viewed in terms of the needs assessment's overall purpose. Since needs assessment is usually a part of a program improvement process, the analysis activities must be conceptualized and conducted in order to provide results that will be valuable to those who will make use of them. Thus, the analyses must be comprehensible to the audiences, answer their questions, and reflect their value perspectives. Often the audiences should be given a significant role in helping to plan the analyses. Overall, the analysis stage must be conceived and conducted in order to insure results that are useful, feasible, ethical, and accurate.

This chapter contains three main sections. The first part explains *preliminary analysis*, in which one delineates the questions to be answered, and organizes, explores, and assesses the available information. Essentially, preliminary analysis involves developing a working knowledge of the existing information, not the collection of new information. The second section discusses *needs and strengths analysis* to identify and diagnose met and unmet needs and to inventory strengths that can be used to address unmet needs. The third section covers *treatments analysis* which is intended to clarify criteria for treatment selection, identify alternative applicable treatments, and rate and rank possible treatments. Each type of analysis is explained, related to relevant techniques, and illustrated. A general case is employed to illustrate the analytic process, and additional examples are used throughout the chapter.

## Preliminary Analysis

In needs assessments, the analysis tasks often are assigned to persons other than those who collected the information. They may be special consultants chosen for their skills in quantitative and qualitative analysis or members of another committee or group. For many reasons, those doing the analysis may initially be unfamiliar with the available information and how and why it was collected. Therefore, before they can proceed with the essential tasks of identifying needs and assessing treatments, they must undertake a preliminary examination of the available information. In particular, they must review the questions to be answered and the available information, insure that the information is organized to promote efficient processing, and assess its adequacy. Below, each of these steps in a preliminary analysis is briefly discussed. The intent is to explain what would be involved if the analyst had to undertake all of these steps. However, in some needs assessments, some or all of these steps could be skipped if they had already been thoroughly addressed in the preparation and/or information-gathering processes, and if those assigned to do the analysis had been involved in those stages. Keeping these comments in mind, we will discuss each of the preliminary analysis steps.

### Review and Clarify the Questions to Be Answered

Obviously, the persons assigned to analyze the needs assessment information must become familiar with the questions to be answered. Moreover, any questions that are cryptic, illogical, or too general should be clarified. Analysts should also establish the relative importance of different questions in case resources and time restrict what can be done. Finally, they should check to insure that the questions included in the previous needs assessment plans are still regarded as appropriate and sufficient. In pursuing this review and clarification activity, the analysts should study key documents such as the needs assessment design, management plan, and contract. They should also, if necessary, discuss the issues with the client and consult representatives of key audiences.

### Explore the Collected Information

Keeping in mind the questions to be answered, the analysts should become familiar with the available information. They should examine it for leads concerning possible needs, conflicting value perspectives, important political factors, distinguishing characteristics of the target population, essential characteristics of existing programs, and so forth. Gaining familiarity with the available information before starting to organize and analyze it can assist the analyst in increasing the sensitivity and relevance of the eventual analyses. In this respect, the analyst is more like a detective looking for clues than a computer technician activating "canned" programs.

### Assemble the Basic Information

Once the analysts have gained familiarity with the information, they should make sure it is appropriately organized. This task may or may not have been fully accomplished during the collection of information stage. The main point is to insure that all of the available information is easy to access.

If these considerations are not addressed, potentially available information may be underutilized or used inefficiently.

The system of filing the information should provide easy access by relevant dimensions of the information as determined in the preliminary investigation. Such dimensions might include some of the following: sources of the information; geographic areas from which the information was provided; dates on which the information was collected; grade levels to which the information applies; and questions for which the information has relevance. The documents can be grouped in any way that is considered convenient and appropriate to the given needs assessment. For example, they might be divided as follows: all newspaper accounts, Fall 1980 test results for each school and grade level, all Individual Education Programs for each school, etc. After outlining the aspects by which the information is to be accessed, each unit of information can be assigned an appropriate code which can be numerical, alphabetical, or a combination of these. Coding in this manner allows, as shown in the following example, easy access to the documents that are required for a particular analysis, easy regrouping for the analysis, and easy replacement in the appropriate folders.

### Coding Example

A needs assessment was conducted in a certain school district, focusing on the students' abilities in the areas of reading, math, writing, and science in grades 7, 9, and 11. The district had 15 buildings in which these grades were located, and these buildings were located in four distinct geographic areas of the city. An example of a coding system for this situation is shown in table 4-1. Math scores of ninth grade students on the standardized test from January of 1980 in building #13 in the north quadrant of the city were coded as follows: procedure, 01; source, 01; curriculum area, M; grades, 9; mo/yr, 01/80; building, 13; geographic area, 01. Code = 01.01.M.09.01/ 80.13.01.

Access to the filed information can be enhanced by appropriate indexing. Each aspect by which information might be retrieved can be recorded on a separate index card (for example, Brown School, Fall 1980 information, Individual Education Programs, fifth grade information, fourth grade information, newspaper accounts, survey results, test results). The numbers of all the folders that contain information on the given aspect can then be written on the card. The cards can then be arranged alphabetically according to the aspect of information identified. Numerical filing coupled

Table 4-1. Example of a Coding System

| Procedure | Source | Curriculum Area | Grades | Mo/Yr | Buildings | Geographic Area |
|---|---|---|---|---|---|---|
| Standardized tests = 01 | Students = 01 | Reading comp = RC | 07 | 01 = January | 1–15 | North = 01 |
| Interviews = 02 | Teachers = 02 | Reading recall = RR | 09 | 12 = December | | West = 02 |
| Teacher tests = 03 | Parents = 03 | Math = M | 11 | Year = 78, 79, 80 | | South = 03 |
| | Principals = 04 | Writing = W | | | | East = 04 |
| | | Science = S | | | | |

115

with an alphabetized index card file is applicable to large as well as small-scale assessments.

## Assessing the Available Information

Once the assessors have explored and organized their base of information, they should assess its adequacy. The adequacy of the resulting information base should be evaluated in relationship to the needs assessment questions, the needs assessment design, and the technical aspects of measurement. The information base can be evaluated by answering the following kinds of questions:

1. Have all data specified in the design been collected?
2. If compromises were made in the design or measurement procedures, how will these affect the resulting information?
3. How were incomplete or invalid responses handled? How will this affect the integrity of the resulting information? Did this procedure result in a biased sample?
4. What information was collected that was not planned for in the needs assessment design?
5. Is additional information required to address the needs assessment question?
6. Is the resulting information sufficient to answer the needs assessment question?
7. What are the characteristics (for example, objectivity, reliability, and validity) of each information set?

The assessment of the evidence should culminate in conclusions and recommendations regarding the technical and substantive adequacy of the existing information and possibly the need to gather additional information. Often, the need to gather more information will require an adjustment in both the time frame and the budget for the needs assessment.

## Preliminary Analysis Illustrated

Four steps in conducting a preliminary analysis of needs assessment information have been listed and described. This section illustrates how these steps might be carried out in a school district needs assessment.

A parent-teacher association (PTA), with the support of their school board and superintendent, decided to do a needs assessment in relation to six elementary schools in their district to identify the areas most needing improvement in the district as a whole and in each school. With the help of the district's evaluation office, the PTA group decided to collect ten kinds of information about the performance of the students in each school: four concerned the student's intellectual development and six concerned their moral, aesthetic, social, vocational, emotional, and physical development. Data were gathered such that at least one variable was assessed in each of the six grade levels. In addition, the PTA collected available information, including cumulative folder information from a stratified random sample of students in each school with the information carefully disguised so that no student could be identified. They also gathered copies of the minutes from past board meetings over the last two years; results from hearings held in each of the six schools; newspaper articles; and official reports concerning a govenrment agency's assessment of the school district in relation to the provisions against desegregation in the Civil Rights Act of 1964; and interviews with each school principal, a sample of ten teachers from each school, and a sample of five parents from each school.

With the help of the school district evaluators, the PTA group filed the obtained information from interviews, cumulative folders, newspapers, and so forth—according to the main data collection procedures. Further, each item of information was assigned an identification number and indexed in a Rolodex card file according to pertinent descriptors such as attendance center, month and year the information was collected, data collection procedure, population sampled, and domain of information.

The PTA group then formed five subgroups. The first was a steering committee to coordinate the other subcommittees (especially in regards to their use of the centralized information system), to review and possibly clarify the questions to be addressed, and to assess the adequacy of the available information. The other subgroups were assigned to investigate the information pertaining to the students in each school, to examine information about the programs of each school, to analyze community context information, and to delineate basic issues and concerns from the available information about elementary education in the district as a whole and in each of its schools. One member from the steering group served on each of the other subcommittees, and the steering group met weekly to share information and problems from the other groups.

At a meeting of the full committee, the steering subcommittee invited all members to review the questions specified at the beginning of the study.

After considerable discussion, the group agreed the original questions were too numerous and specific and decided that answering all of them was neither necessary nor feasible. Subsequently, the group agreed on four general questions:

1. What level of attainment should be set as the district-wide goal for each of the developmental variables that were selected for use in the assessment?
2. What is the current level of attainment on the variables in each elementary school?
3. What factors might explain performance in a school that is substantially above or below the district-wide standard?
4. What steps can be taken to improve the pattern of performance in each school?

Although the group realized that the questions were general and perhaps too few in number, they agreed that, for the time being, these questions were the most important and would provide an adequate focus for the subsequent analysis. They also agreed that each subcommittee should feel free to list additional questions, particularly the subcommittee assigned to identify issues and concerns.

When the subcommittee on issues and concerns met, they examined the information base in order to identify community members' concerns, especially those that were controversial. Each concern was listed and described, and a listing of information available in the filing system on each concern was provided along with a summary of the implications of the available information. The concerns included in this report were as follows: safety, busing, quality of education, legality of the existing program, value conflicts regarding the goals and objectives of education in the community, and finances. Whenever possible, the report referred to the different positions on each of these concerns held by various population samples (for example, each minority parent group, building administrators, students, teachers, members of the professional community); and sources of information, especially interview and hearing results.

The subcommittee on students reviewed the attendance, demographic, and achievement records for the district as a whole and for each of the elementary schools. For the district as a whole, they identified trends of declining enrollment, increasing percentage of minority students, declining dropout rates, declining scores on nationally standardized tests, and increasing attendance rates. For the six elementary schools, they noted an uneven distribution of minority students and considerable disparity in achievement on nationally standardized tests. In general, this subcommittee concluded that there was considerable need for improvement of student performance for the district as a whole and for at least four of the elementary schools.

The subcommittee on program produced a report summarizing the available information about the programs operating in each of the six elementary schools. Basically, the description for each school included the school schedule of activities, the characterization of the curriculum guides for different subject matter areas, programs for a sample of individual students, a characterization of the philosphies and goals of the total elementary school program as provided by the school principal, a summary of the findings of a North Central committee report regarding programs in each school, and a description of comments and judgments about the program in each school made by the various groups that participated in the interviews and hearings. Finally, the program description paper included a summary of the government investigator's preliminary findings regarding the status of integration in each of the schools, a characterization of the school district's plan for busing students to increase integration, and an assessment of how that plan would affect the population in each of the elementary schools.

The subcommittee on context prepared a report that summarized the available information regarding the community setting in which the six elementary schools were operating. Particularly prominent in that report were the positions various groups in the community were taking toward the proposed integration plan for the school district. The report summarized the information available about the federal government investigation; reviewed the conflicting positions of different members of the school board on the busing issue; provided a summary of items appearing in local newspapers; summarized available information concerning charges that the integration plan was leading to "white flight"; presented data on enrollment trends in the private schools; and summarized the results of hearings in each of the school's attendance areas, particularly in reference to opinions about the quality of education in the school and comments about the desegregation/busing issue. Overall, then, the report on context summarized community assessments of the school programs and of the busing situation by attendance area.

When the subcommittees had completed the work described above, they met to share and discuss their findings. Following their discussion of the reports, the group agreed they were now better informed about the school district and, consequently, better prepared to proceed with the subsequent analysis. They saw the information as rich, multifaceted, frank, and unbiased and agreed that it provided a sufficient basis for proceeding with the analysis. Much of the information was not directly related to the four questions they had chosen to address. However, all of the information was viewed generally relevant for developing interpretations and for helping the audience for their report to interpret its findings and recommendations in relation to the community context. In short, they felt the preliminary analysis had helped them gain *a much better understanding* of the school district.

They next turned to the difficult task of determining appropriate attainment levels for each of the developmental variables chosen for use in the assessment. They reviewed the data collection instruments for each variable, consulted with the professional educators in their group, and reviewed normative data available for the instruments. They then heard and voted on motions regarding performance standards to be used in further analysis work. At the end of the meeting, the group generally agreed that they felt uncomfortable about the standards selected and acknowledged they should use them cautiously. They agreed, however, that the standards reflected their best judgments and should prove useful in interpreting and comparing student performance in each school.

Having set tentative standards, the group next outlined the steps that should be pursued in the analyses to answer the four general questions they had agreed to address. They wanted (1) to see each school's average performance on each of the performance variables; (2) to compare the each school's performance on each variable with the standard set for the variable; and (3) to see some kind of score or summary assessment for each school that reflected the quality of its overall educational program. They then asked the district's evaluator to perform analyses that were responsive to these requirements.

The evaluator complimented the members of the group for doing their homework and getting straight to the point of what they wanted from him. He said he thought he had enough guidance for the time being to address their concerns. He added that he would do analyses beyond those requested to help them look at the variability of performance within schools as well as the variance among the schools. He said he was not confident that he could compute single scores to reflect the overall quality of a school program, but that he would work on the problem. He also predicted that the results of these analyses would likely evoke additional questions that would require further analysis and possibly more data collection. He pointed out that the reports they had already prepared regarding their investigation of the available information would likely be very useful in interpreting the results of his analyses and in performing further, more diagnostic investigations.

He concluded by saying that he would schedule a meeting with them as soon as the first analyses were completed, probably in about two weeks.

This example illustrates how a group might explore and assess the available information and how they might focus the main analysis task. It illustrates as well that there is much that groups lacking technical sophistication in statistics can do to investigate available information. And, it shows that analysis is an exploratory process: initial questions are considered; available information is examined; more questions come to mind, leading to further examination, and perhaps the collection of additional information. Also, the example reflects the fact that analysis is an inexact activity, since standards often must be invoked to proceed with interpretation, but all standards in varying degrees are arbitrary.

*An Overview of Analysis Tasks*

The preceding illustration reflects our basic position that there are four underlying questions to be addressed by analysis in any educational needs assessment. Paraphrased from the summary of chapter 1, they are: (1) What educational outcomes are desired? (2) Which ones are and are not being achieved? (3) What factors might explain both substandard and superior performance? and (4) What can be done to sustain acceptable performance and to improve substandard performance?

Analyses to address these four questions are summarized in table 4-2. The questions form the column headings of the table. The row headings are four issues that relate to each question: the types of information that might be available for analysis, the purpose of the analysis, the basic assumptions to guide the analysis, and relevant techniques. This table summarizes the contents of the remainder of this chapter. Techniques to address the first three questions are discussed in the second section of this chapter, "Strengths and Needs Analysis." Techniques to address the fourth question are described in the last section, "Treatment Analysis." Techniques included in table 4-2, but not discussed in the two sections mentioned above, are illustrated in Appendix B.

**Needs and Strengths Analysis**

Once the preliminary work has been completed, the analysts can turn to the fundamental tasks of identifying needs and strengths. These tasks are depicted in columns 1, 2, and 3 of table 4-2, and are explained in the remainder of this section.

Table 4-2. An Overview of the Analysis of Needs Assessment Information

| | Questions to Guide Analysis of Needs and Strengths Assessment Information | | | |
| --- | --- | --- | --- | --- |
| | 1. What educational outcomes are desired? | 2. Which desired outcomes are and are not being achieved? | 3. What factors might explain acceptable and unacceptable performance? | 4. What could be done to sustain or improve acceptable performance and to improve substandard performance? |
| Types of information to be analyzed | Mission statements, lesson plans, goals, collective judgments of desired performance levels, position papers, policies, minutes of meetings, laws, court rulings, survey results, and individual educational plans | Test scores, activity records, school records, school population characteristics, grades, committee reports, survey results, crime statistics, employer judgments, and post–secondary school academic records | Attendance records, socioeconomic data, site visit reports, test data, cumulative folder information, classroom observation reports, time study reports, school climate reports, and educational theory | Budget and expenditure reports, research articles, reviews of research, reports of visits to other districts, consultant reports, accreditation reports, court rulings, and advocacy team proposals |
| Purpose of the Analysis | To identify and contrast competing views of what outcomes are | To assess, summarize, and interpret descriptive and judgmental | To formulate and assess hypotheses about what strengths | To identify and assess competing proposals for addressing both |

|  | | | | |
|---|---|---|---|---|
|  | desirable for groups, subgroups, and individuals | information so as to contrast performance with purpose for groups, subgroups, and individuals | and weaknesses in the school programs are associated with both acceptable and unacceptable performance | met and unmet needs and provide recommendations for resource acquisition and resource allocation |
| Guiding assumptions | Desired outcomes may legitimately differ as a function of value perspective and individual differences | Alternative analyses will usually be required to take account of relevant value perspectives and individual differences | Ideally, causal explanations should be developed; realistically, however, the available information usually will permit only reasoned interpretations | Before converging on a solution strategy, alternative possibilities should be examined for their feasibility in meeting the needs of groups, subgroups, and individuals |
| Relevant techniques | Content analysis, Delphi technique, system analysis, expert review, and judicial hearings. | Descriptive statistics, analysis of variance, a posteriori analysis, committee review, norm referenced analysis, objectives referenced analysis, and goal-scale analysis | Discriminant function analysis, committee review, a posteriori analysis, meta analysis, effect parameter analysis, and modus operandi analysis | Advocacy teams, adversary/advocacy reviews, sociodrama, and cost analysis |

## Identifying Desired Outcomes

According to the definition used in this book, a *need* is something that is necessary or useful for fulfilling some defensible purpose. The fundamental concept in this definition—as explained in chapter 1—is defensible purpose. Claims that some levels of achievement and some specified action are needed can be defended only if these alleged needs can be shown to contribute to meeting some worthy purpose. For this reason, primary concerns in the analysis of needs assessment information are to identify the purpose to be served by identifying and meeting needs, and to assess how the fulfillment of this purpose will benefit or harm individuals, groups, and society at large. Needs assessors should have these concerns in mind when they address the first general question in table 4-2: What educational outcomes are desired?

Information that pertains to this question might be of several kinds—a mission statement, a set of goal statements, collective judgments of desired performance levels, or one or more position papers. It could include public policies, laws, and court rulings. And it could include individual educational plans, lesson plans, minutes of meetings, or survey results. Such items of information might emanate from a variety of sources (such as a school board, teachers, parents, students, and experts) and might reflect a wide range of performance dimensions (intellectual, emotional, social, moral, physical, vocational, and aesthetic). The pertinent information should be analyzed to identify and contrast competing views of what outcomes are desirable. Often it should be examined so as to discern whether different outcomes should be sought for different subgroups or even individuals. In general, the analyses should help the audience for the needs assessment see agreements and disagreements about what outcomes are to be desired for a total group and its subgroups and individual members.

This position assumes that desired educational outcomes may legitimately differ as a function of value perspective and of the individual differences among students. Therefore, the needs assessors have an obligation to help their audience view complexity and diversity before they take a position that posits a certain set of desired educational outcomes. The defense of this position rests in the facts that schools serve a pluralistic society and that students vary considerably in aptitudes and interests. Generally, a single set of goals, and especially performance levels, is not appropriate for all members of a group.

The information that may be used to identify and assess the desirability of educational outcomes is mainly qualitative in nature. As shown in table 4-2, a variety of techniques are especially useful for analyzing this information, including content analysis, Delphi technique, system analysis, expert review, and judicial hearings.

## Determining Met and Unmet Primary Needs

In this book, *primary needs* are considered the human conditions that must be satisfied in order for a defensible purpose to be fulfilled. If the defensible purpose is to develop functional literacy in all students in a school, then the primary needs could include the abilities to read, write, and compute, at least to the level of proficiency required to function satisfactorily in the local social environment. The statements of primary needs are basically derived from statements of purpose and from relevant theory and research that explicate the purpose. They usually include judgments about what levels of performance are acceptable or desirable.

Information concerning whether the primary needs are met or unmet is obtained from a variety of sources, for example, test scores, activity records, school population characteristics, grades, committee reports, survey results, crime statistics, employer judgments, and post–secondary school academic records. These are just some of the information items that may be available and useful in determining the extent to which desired outcomes are and are not being achieved. This information is descriptive, as well as judgmental, qualitative as well as quantitative.

The main purpose of analyzing such information is to assess, summarize, and interpret it so performance can be compared with purpose. Moreover, this analysis typically should provide separate results for groups, sub-groups, and individuals because all people will not have the same pattern of met and unmet needs. In general, the purpose of the analyses in identifying met and unmet needs is to help the audience both identify sound achievements that need to be sustained and set goals and priorities for improvement efforts.

The analysis should take into account the different value perspectives of the audience. The assessors should keep in mind that it will often be appropriate to conduct alternative analyses that might give different answers to the general question of what needs are and are not being met because the different audiences might have different convictions about what levels of performance on the various dimensions of primary need should be considered acceptable. Another reason for conducting alternative analyses is that different subgroups and students will have different backgrounds, levels of aspiration, and aptitudes. Using one standard of performance for all of them would surely be a disservice to some of them.

Generally, the assessors should consult representatives of the different reference groups and carefully consider the characteristics of the people whose primary needs are to be assessed as they plan how they will analyze the information that has been collected.

Many techniques are available for use in analyzing this information. Those deemed most applicable are descriptive statistics, analysis of variance, a posteriori analysis, committee review, norm-referenced analysis, objectives-referenced analysis, and goal-scale analysis.

### Identifying Secondary Needs

A position emphasized in this book is that the fulfillment of primary needs requires that certain functional secondary enabling needs be met. In the language of research, the primary needs are the dependent variables, whereas the secondary needs are independent variables. For example, ability to read newspapers might be the primary need or dependent variable, and good vision and effective reading instruction might then be identified as two of the crucial secondary needs or independent variables. Crucial analytic tasks in needs assessment involve discerning which secondary needs must be satisfied in order to meet the primary needs and then discovering which secondary needs are not being met. This is a kind of diagnostic activity that culminates in a set of instrumental objectives, that is, objectives that have to be achieved in order to meet the primary needs and thereby help fulfill the defensible purpose.

In educational needs assessment, a variety of sources of information can be used to investigate secondary needs. One crucial source is educational theory, which examines hypotheses and supporting evidence about which conditions, capacities, experiences, resources, and so forth, are linked to achievements in given areas. Exploration of this source is especially important in searching for hypotheses about what is necessary and useful for fulfilling given primary needs. Other sources of information can then be used to check whether the hypothesized secondary needs are being met in the given situation. These sources include socioeconomic data, site visitor reports, test item data, cumulative folder information, classroom observation reports, time study reports, and school climate reports, among others.

Ideally, cause-and-effect relationships between secondary and primary needs would be explored as a part of a needs assessment. For example, the needs assessment data could come from true experiments in which the primary needs of equivalent groups had been assessed after the groups had received different levels of assistance in the areas of the hypothesized secondary needs. However, only rarely do needs assessors have access to information of this type. Realistically, they usually will not be able to establish empirically the causal links between the primary needs and the hypothesized secondary needs. However, needs assessors can consult relevant theory, invoke common sense, and carefully examine the available evidence to develop reasonable interpretations and recommendations. Techniques that can be used to develop the conclusions include literature review, experiments, Delphi technique, and modus operandi analysis.

## Needs-and-Strengths Analysis Illustrated

At this point, we will continue the story of the analysis of information from six elementary schools intended to help the PTA group identify school level needs. The story was told to the point where the PTA group had commissioned the school district's evaluator to help them answer their basic questions by analyzing the available information. Those questions were:

1. What level of attainment should be set as the district-wide goal for each of the ten developmental variables that were selected for use in the assessment?
2. What is the current level of attainment on the ten variables in each elementary school?
3. What factors might explain performance in a school that is substantially above or below the district-wide standard?
4. What steps can be taken to improve the pattern of performance in each school?

In considering the first question, the evaluator recalled that the PTA group was unsure of the adequacy of the performance levels they had set for each of the variables. Realizing that little of the information available for analysis was directly related to this question, he decided to collect some additional information. He asked the principal in each of the six schools to assist by convening a group of 12 people, including six teachers and six parents. Each group was asked to review definitions of the ten variables and the instruments and procedures used to gather information about the students' performance on the variables. Then each group was guided through two exercises: one designed to rate the relative importance of each variable, the other to reach agreements about desired performance level of a school as a whole on each variable. The first of these exercises consisted of having each member of a group divide 100 points among the ten variables. In the second exercise, the members of each group completed two or three rounds of a Delphi study until they had reached a consensus on the performance level for each variable that they thought would be appropriate for the students in their school.

The evaluator summarized and analyzed the results of each exercise. He incorporated the findings into an interim report and met with the PTA group to discuss the report. He first directed their attention to the issue of the relative importance of the variables they had chosen. He noted that he had collected judgments from groups of six parents and six teachers in each school and referred them to a table which summarized the collected judgments (table 4-3). This table contains means and standard deviations, by school, of the number of points out of 100 that had been allocated to each variable.

The PTA group asked the evaluator to summarize the meaning of the table for the district as a whole. In response to their request, he computed the overall average number of points allocated to each variable, but stressed that differences between schools should also be taken into account. He then reported the following overall averages calculated from the individual school averages of points allocated to each variable:

| Variable | Average No. Points Assigned |
|---|---|
| 1. Percentage of second grade students judged by their teachers as emotionally healthy | 10.75 |
| 2. Percentage of crime-free days during prior year | 9.35 |
| 3. Percentage of sixth grade students passing district vocational maturity test | 9.42 |
| 4. Percentage of fifth grade students judged to be meaningfully engaged in aesthetic activity | 9.25 |
| 5. Congruence between school and district student bodies on percentage low-income families (district average = 20%). | 10.12 |
| 6. Percentage of sixth grade students passing district's physical fitness test | 9.90 |
| 7. Percentage of fourth grade students passing state reading exam | 11.03 |
| 8. Percent of fourth grade students passing state arithmetic exam | 10.78 |
| 9. Percent of third grade students passing district's writing exam | 9.58 |

10. Percent of first grade students passing district's
    science exam                                                     9.82

After considerable discussion, the PTA group agreed that there were no startling variations in the judgments that had been collected. They decided that for purposes of further analysis, the variables should be treated as equally important.

The evaluator then directed the group's attention to the results of the six Delphi studies that had been conducted (table 4-4). The PTA group observed there was considerable agreement across schools and proceeded to determine a district-wide standard for each school to aid in interpreting the results for the district as a whole and for each school. The performance standards listed below were a result of this process:

1. *100 percent* of the second grade students should be judged emotionally healthy.
2. There should be *100 percent* crime-free days during a school year.
3. At least *90 percent* of sixth grade students should pass the district's vocational maturity test.
4. *100 percent* of fifth grade students should be judged to be meaningfully engaged in an aesthetic activity at least *40* minutes per week.
5. Each school should include at least *15 percent* and not more than *25 percent* students from low-income families.
6. At least *80 percent* of sixth grade students should pass the district's physical fitness exam.
7. At least *95 percent* of fourth grade students should pass the state reading exam.
8. At least *95 percent* of fourth grade students should pass the state arithmetic exam.
9. At least *90 percent* of third grade students should pass the district's writing exam.
10. At least *90 percent* of first grade students should pass the district's science exam.

At this point the evaluator and the PTA group agreed that they had completed what they had set out to do in determining performance standards for the *developmental* variables.

The evaluator then directed his analyses to their second question— assessing the current level of attainment on each dependent variable. At the next meeting the evaluator presented the information summarized in figure 4-1. The variables on which data were gathered are listed down the side and

Table 4-3. Allocation of 100 Points Among Ten Developmental Variables to Reflect Their Relative Importance by Six Parents and Six Teachers in Each School

| Variable | Brown | | Hays | | Jones | | Smith | | Henry | | Foster | |
|---|---|---|---|---|---|---|---|---|---|---|---|---|
| | $\bar{X}$ | S | $\bar{X}$ | S | $\bar{X}$ | S | $\bar{X}$ | S | $\bar{X}$ | S | $\bar{X}$ | S |
| 1. Percentage of 2nd grade students judged emotionally healthy | 15.1 | 2.2 | 10.2 | 1.7 | 11.7 | 0.9 | 9.7 | 0.7 | 8.7 | 0.8 | 9.1 | 1.6 |
| 2. Percentage of crime-free days during prior year | 7.2 | 1.7 | 9.7 | 1.1 | 8.8 | 1.3 | 9.1 | 1.6 | 10.7 | 0.9 | 10.6 | 1.4 |
| 3. Percentage of 6th grade students passing district vocational maturity test | 6.4 | 1.6 | 8.6 | 0.9 | 10.1 | 0.7 | 9.7 | 1.3 | 11.0 | 1.1 | 10.7 | 1.0 |
| 4. Percentage of 5th grade students judged to be meaningfully engaged in aesthetic activity | 5.1 | 2.3 | 9.1 | 1.7 | 10.3 | 1.6 | 8.3 | 1.2 | 12.2 | 0.9 | 10.5 | 1.3 |
| 5. Congruence between school and district student bodies on percent of low-income families (district average = 20%) | 10.1 | 1.2 | 8.1 | 0.8 | 8.1 | 1.7 | 12.1 | 0.8 | 11.2 | 1.2 | 11.1 | 1.1 |
| 6. Percentage of 6th grade students passing district's physical fitness test | 9.2 | 2.2 | 8.3 | 1.3 | 8.1 | 2.1 | 12.5 | 0.7 | 10.8 | 1.4 | 10.5 | 1.3 |
| 7. Percentage of 4th grade students passing state reading exam | 14.3 | 1.0 | 11.7 | 0.6 | 12.0 | 0.4 | 10.2 | 1.3 | 8.2 | 1.1 | 9.8 | 1.1 |

Table 4-3.

| Variable | Brown | | Hays | | Jones | | Smith | | Henry | | Foster | |
|---|---|---|---|---|---|---|---|---|---|---|---|---|
| | $\bar{X}$ | S | $\bar{X}$ | S | $\bar{X}$ | S | $\bar{X}$ | S | $\bar{X}$ | S | $\bar{X}$ | S |
| 8. Percentage of 4th grade students passing state arithmetic exam | 13.1 | 0.7 | 12.1 | 0.5 | 10.6 | 0.7 | 8.6 | 1.5 | 9.2 | 1.2 | 11.1 | 0.9 |
| 9. Percentage of 3rd grade students passing district's writing exam | 10.4 | 1.4 | 9.7 | 0.9 | 10.8 | 1.1 | 8.1 | 1.1 | 10.6 | 0.8 | 7.9 | 1.0 |
| 10. Percentage of 1st grade students passing district's science exam | 9.1 | 1.5 | 12.5 | 0.7 | 9.5 | 0.9 | 11.7 | 1.0 | 7.4 | 1.4 | 8.7 | 1.0 |
| Total points | 100 | | 100 | | 100 | | 100 | | 100 | | 100 | |

131

Table 4-4.  Results of Delphi Studies in Six Schools to Set Performance Standards

| Variable | Brown | Hays | Jones | Smith | Henry | Foster |
|---|---|---|---|---|---|---|
| 1. Percentage of 2nd grade students judged emotionally healthy | 95 | 100 | 100 | 98 | 96 | 100 |
| 2. Percentage of crime-free days during prior year. | 90 | 99 | 100 | 100 | 98 | 100 |
| 3. Percentage of 6th grade students passing district vocational maturity test. | 85 | 95 | 90 | 91 | 89 | 90 |
| 4. Percentage of 5th grade students judged to be meaningfully engaged in aesthetic activity | 100 | 100 | 95 | 100 | 100 | 100 |
| 5. Congruence between school and district student bodies on percentage of low-income families (district average = 20%) | ± 5% difference | ± 5% difference | ± 5% difference | ± 5% difference | ± 5% difference | ± 5% difference |
| 6. Percentage of 6th grade students passing district's physical fitness test | 90 | 95 | 94 | 95 | 95 | 100 |
| 7. Percentage of 4th grade students passing state reading exam | 90 | 94 | 96 | 95 | 95 | 95 |
| 8. Percentage of 4th grade students passing state arithmetic exam | 95 | 90 | 92 | 95 | 98 | 96 |
| 9. Percentage of 3rd grade students passing district's writing exam | 85 | 90 | 92 | 90 | 89 | 90 |
| 10. Percentage of 1st grade students passing district's science exam | 85 | 92 | 90 | 90 | 89 | 90 |

the district ideal plus the names of the six elementary schools are listed across the bottom. The maximum range of each variable according to the limit of the district ideal is represented by a given distance, approximately 1/2 of an inch; and the results for each school are represented in the form of a cumulative bar graph, with a maximum height of about 3 1/2 inches. The

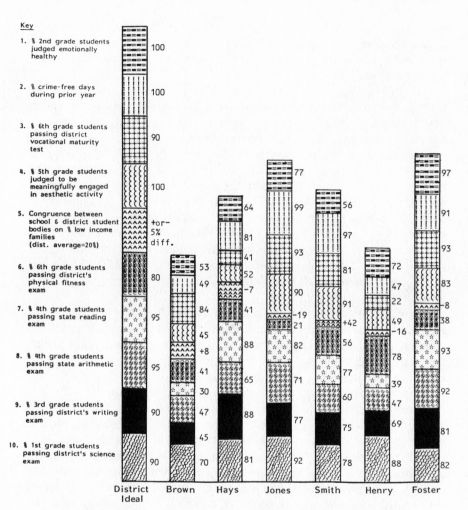

Figure 4-1.  Indicators of Educational Development in the Elementary Schools of the Black River School District

results show: (1) no school's overall performance matches the district standards; (2) children from low-income families are distributed quite unevenly throughout the district; (3) at least one school surpasses or comes close to matching the district-wide standard for all variables except number 5, composition of the student body; (4) Smith School is noteworthy for its consistently strong showing in spite of the fact that half of its students come from underprivileged homes; (5) Henry School's overall performance appears low, especially since only four percent of its student body comes from underprivileged homes; and (6) every school has a strong showing on at least one variable.

The study group met with the PTA group of each school to explain the results in figure 4-1, and to consider their implications for program improvement. In each case, the discussion of the findings raised more questions than were answered. For example, the group at Jones School wanted to know whether their school's low showing on the physical fitness test reflected a lack of attention to this area. The groups at Brown and Henry Schools wondered whether their school spent as much time on reading as did the other schools. The group at Hayes raised questions about their teachers' qualifications to teach art, music, drama, and dance. With the help of the central PTA team and the district evaluator, a study team was formed at each school. Each team investigated questions that were of interest to the teachers, parents, and principals in the school. The intent was to diagnose problems whose solutions would lead to improved performances in the local school.

A similar investigation was launched at the district level. The superintendent, concerned about the uneven distribution of underprivileged children and the uneven performance of the six schools in the district, directed the district evaluator to identify any instances of unequal educational opportunity in the district. In responding to this charge, the evaluator assembled the information appearing in table 4-5. He also reviewed the results of the hearings that had been conducted in each of the six schools, interviewed representatives from each schools' study team, and analyzed samples of teachers' lesson plans and of students' cumulative records for each school. The results appeared in a written report that was presented to the school superintendent and distributed to the teachers, parents, and administrators involved in the study. Moreover, a version of the report was also presented at a meeting of the superintendent's cabinet.

Based on the results, the superintendent concluded that both educational achievement and opportunity were too unequal among the six schools. He decided with the board's concurrence to launch a program of educational reform in the elementary schools and to seek an outside grant to support the program. In accordance with this decision, he charged the district's director of elementary education and the evaluator to prepare an appropriate plan. The new program was to achieve the following: (1) upgrade the overall performance of Brown and Henry Schools, (2) preserve and strengthen the good performance in the other four schools, (3) insure that

Table 4-5.   Indicators of Educational Opportunity in the Elementary Schools of the Black River School District

|  | *Brown* | *Hays* | *Jones* | *Smith* | *Henry* | *Foster* |
|---|---|---|---|---|---|---|
| 1. Hours per week of psychological services available to the school | 4 | 12 | 12 | 12 | 5 | 12 |
| 2. Hours per week per grade devoted to the district's character education program | 0 | 2 | 2 | 4 | 1 | 1½ |
| 3. Hours per week devoted to vocational education (6th grade) | 1 | 2 | 2 | 1½ | 1 | 2 |
| 4. Total hours per week of aesthetics education instruction (5th grade) | 6 | 4 | 12 | 10 | 5 | 10 |
| 5. Hours per week devoted physical fitness (6th grade) | 1½ | 1½ | 1 | 2½ | 6 | 1½ |
| 6. Hours per week devoted to reading (4th grade) | 2½ | 5 | 5 | 4 | 5 | 6 |
| 7. Hours per week devoted to arithmetic (4th grade) | 1½ | 3 | 4 | 2 | 5 | 4 |
| 8. Hours per week devoted to writing (3rd grade) | 1 | 3 | 3 | 2 | 3 | 3 |
| 9. Hours per week devoted to science (1st grade) | 1 | 2 | 2½ | 1½ | 2 | 2½ |
| 10. Average years experience of teachers | 2 | 5½ | 8 | 3½ | 4 | 7 |
| 11. Average no. semester hours earned by teachers | 127 | 139 | 147 | 135 | 123 | 148 |

educational services are equally available in all of the schools, (4) obtain a more even mix of children of varying socioeconomic levels at each school, and (5) involve persons from all of the schools in planning the program.

## Treatments Analysis

Thus far the interplay between theory and practice in the foregoing material illustrates that needs analyses involve assembling the available information, getting a clear grasp on the questions to be addressed, and analyzing the basic information to help the audience reach some conclusion about unmet needs, strengths to be built upon, and objectives to be pursued. The remainder of the chapter deals with the issue of identifying and assessing solution strategies (or treatments).

It is debatable whether treatments analysis is actually a part of needs assessment, but perhaps it is a disservice to separate these two activities, since the search for alternative solutions is often inherent in the assessment of performance deficits. It will make little difference that needs and strengths were identified and objectives specified if some systematic effort is not made to identify how best to meet the specified objectives and thereby to satisfy the identified needs.

In most circumstances, particularly in educational settings, it is misleading to refer to this step as *choosing* a solution strategy from among a pool of potential contenders. Most often, there will be no complete solution strategy already available for educational decision-makers to choose, much less a pool of such strategies. The problems identified by the needs assessment are complex and interrelated, and their specific causes will rarely be accurately and completely understood. To some extent, they exist in part because there is no comprehensive, formal solution. Had such a solution been readily available, the problem might not have arisen. Thus, this step may be thought of as a creative decision-making process whereby. one investigates strategies and approaches used in the past for similar kinds of problems, and develops a sort of "hybrid" program that, considering the peculiarities of the present situation, looks as if it might work. In the remainder of this chapter, procedures for delineating a promising strategy for meeting identified educational needs are presented and discussed.

Basically, treatments analysis involves the identification and assessment of competing treatments, given a set of needs, strengths, and objectives. A basic approach is to search for other relevant programs in the literature or in other school districts and to characterize and assess them; first, in relation to how well they respond to the district's objectives, needs, and strengths; and second, in terms of how well they would fit with the existing curriculum, how politically viable they would be, and how feasible they are for implementation.

### Criteria for Rating Treatments

An ongoing concern in the search for and assessment of treatments is the identification and clarification of appropriate criteria. This involves identifying the desired characteristics of, and necessary constraints that might impinge on, a program designed to meet the needs. It also involves researching the history of, and knowledge derived from, earlier attempts to address needs of the type identified. Educational decision-makers should be aware of this information in order to understand what might be required to address the identified needs. That is, the criteria to be applied to any program alternative to address a certain need must not only be derived from the context of the potential program environment, but must also be tempered by an understanding of what is required to deal with needs of the kind identified—an understanding of the current state-of-the-art and science regarding that type of need. It should also be noted that the needs assessment data themselves should be consulted in generating criteria. Hopefully, the needs assessment has produced an enriched understanding of school problems and conditions. This knowledge should be used as it represents the most up-to-date assessment of the context in which any new program must operate.

Some categories within which criteria should be developed and applied are listed as follows:

1. *Feasibility*. This includes dollar costs, time demands on participants, material and equipment demands, facilities and space, special conditions, etc.
2. *Validity*. This refers to the projected potency of a program; how ably can it meet an addressed need?
3. *Marketability*. How attractive is a program to concerned consumers or investors?
4. *Political and social viability*. What social, traditional, or political factors impinge?
5. *Legality*. Are there local, state, and federal laws or guidelines to which a program for this need must adhere?
6. *Compatibility*. With what other programs, curricula, or conditions must the new program coexist? What are the demands or limits of coexistence?

## Identifying Treatments

The search for treatments should help the decision-makers become aware of a broad range of alternative strategies for dealing with the identified needs. It is important to note that the spirit of this step is nonjudgmental; it aims to "leave no stone unturned" in the quest for possible approaches to meeting the need. The purpose is not to apply criteria, but to determine as many objects as possible to which the criteria may be applied.

The procedures involved to identify a range of alternative strategies would vary in scope and intensity relative to the level of specificity of the needs assessment and the identified needs. If the needs identified pertain to a single, relatively narrow and specific type of school outcome or condition (such as a need for increased vocabulary acquisition among elementary pupils or increasing participation in athletic activities), then the search for treatment alternatives may be proportionally narrow in scope. If, on the other hand, the needs assessors have identified a set of needs that are more general and varied, the search for alternative approaches will have to be broader in scope and may need to be divided according to categories of needs identified. If, for instance, the needs assessment isolates programmatic needs to increase achievement, decrease vandalism, and improve home-school relations, then the search for possible programs to reach these goals would have to be far-ranging. It is also more likely, with these broader sorts of needs, that there would be fewer options available in the form of curriculum packages or prefabricated programs. For these reasons, several different search procedures might be required. In any case, whether the needs are homogeneous and specific or broad and varied, as many alternative treatment strategies as possible should be identified so that decision-makers may have a realm of options to consider and may be relatively assured that no important option was overlooked.

There are several means by which the search for solution alternatives can be carried out. Several of these are listed and described below. It should be noted that the nature and extent of any of these procedures could vary from limited and cursory to extensive and detailed and that more than one of these procedures might be used at once.

*Current practices research*: Libraries, resource centers, and other information depositories (for example, the National Diffusion Network) are consulted to gather descriptions of strategies for meeting the needs identified.

*Surveys*: This entails mail or telephone questionnaires or interviews of relevant practitioners and others to determine how they have addressed or are currently addressing similar needs in their work.

*Visits*: Trips are made to other districts or areas where programs dealing with identified problems can be seen and discussed with practitioners.

*Consultation with experts*: Experts are contacted to provide opinions and knowledge from experience in fields related to the needs.

*Public forums and meetings*: Problem descriptions are provided to groups to solicit opinions and ideas about possible treatment strategies. In this case, one is interested in drawing out advocacy positions as well as innovative treatment strategies.

*"Brainstorming" sessions*: Small groups of experts or other practitioners are formed to create and list possible strategies. This technique especially requires that a nonjudgmental posture be maintained.

*Requests for proposal*: The district describes the problem and sponsors a "contest" to solicit ideas for relevant programs.

*Advocacy team technique*: Given a set of needs, objectives, and background data, two or more teams are recruited to reflect distinctive philosophical and/or theoretical positions and to construct the strongest competing proposals they can for meeting the given objectives and needs and building on the given strengths.

All of the above listed procedures except the last, advocacy teams, are extensively utilized and should be familiar to the reader. Since advocacy teams may not be familiar, a brief description and explanation of the technique is warranted. The technique was specifically developed to aid in the invention of new alternative programs. The procedure builds on the notions of competition and exploiting rather than avoiding biased positions. In this procedure, teams are provided with all of the background information available on the subject at hand. They are given a structure within which to develop their proposals, indicating what information will be necessary for rating and choosing the alternatives, and they are cued to the criteria that will be used to judge the competing alternatives. As discussed above, these criteria are derived from the previously determined needs and objectives and also reflect more generic concerns such as political viability, feasibility, and legality. Once the competing alternatives are produced, an assessment team is convened to apply the prespecified criteria. Quite often a convergence team composed of members of the teams developing the competing strategies plus other personnel from the setting where implementation is to occur is convened and directed to develop a strategy that merges the best features of the competing strategies and to operationalize the proposed strategy for implementation.

### Rating and Ranking Treatments

In general, the selection of a treatment from the alternatives under consideration involves rating each of the treatment alternatives against the selected criteria. In addition to knowing the criteria, the needs assessor also must have sufficient knowledge of each solution alternative to be able to adequately apply the criteria. This requires considerable definition of each treatment alternative, which can be quite laborious and time-consuming. The nature and extent of this process will, of course, depend on the number of initial solution alternatives.

The key characteristic, which discriminates this step from the previous one, is the application of judgmental criteria. Whereas the previous step is intended to make the field of treatment alternatives as broad as possible, the purpose of this step is to narrow that field. It is probably best to reduce lengthy lists of alternatives through some cursory analysis against the criteria. There may be some alternatives that, despite a very brief description, could be eliminated because they violate particularly crucial criteria (cost, effectiveness, etc.). When obviously unacceptable alternatives are eliminated, the remaining alternatives will require further definition and description before meaningful judgments can be made. Although the amount of information required to make a sound choice will vary according to the criteria to be applied and the magnitude of needs identified, we suggest that information about each treatment alternative be provided in each of the following categories:

*Resources needed*: What are the dollar, staff, facility, equipment, material, and other requirements of the program?

*Preconditions*: What administrative, cooperative, political, legal, social, or other arrangements or conditions are necessary for the program to be installed?

*Activities*: What processes, interactions, and functions are required by the program? These should be described for major components (such as training, instruction, development, counseling) of the program and should identify roles to be played in each by pupils, administrators, teachers, parents, and others.

*Intended outcomes*: What are the expected educational benefits of the program? These should be listed as specifically as possible for each target group (pupils, parents, staff, etc.).

*Side-effects*: What unintended benefits or deficits might accrue if the program were installed?

*Displacement/opportunity effects*: What might need to be curtailed, abandoned, or foregone if this program were installed?

The information defined above constitutes a *program description*. These descriptions are to be judged against the identified criteria. The goal of the judging process may be to identify the single most desirable program, or it may be to identify key strengths and weaknesses of each program alternative so that a feasible and promising program might be constructed. Several techniques are available for both constructing program descriptions and for judging their adequacy against the defined criteria. Although the several techniques defined below are neither exhaustive nor mutually exclusive, they represent a range of possible methods from which a suitable procedure might be developed.

*Hearings and forums*: The program description alternatives and criteria are presented to public groups or meetings of practitioners who then are polled for opinions and judgments regarding the most desirable alternative.

*Juries*: Panels of concerned practitioners, experts, or others are formed and presented with the competing program descriptions. A "judge" presides over the process, and the jury reaches a "verdict" on which program, or program elements, should be employed.

*Expert ratings*: Selected experts, provided with the program descriptions, are asked to rate each according to the prescribed criteria.

*Group decision-making*: A group is formed or identified that will have decision (or recommendation)-making power. The group then considers the program descriptions against the criteria. The group may be empowered to reach a decision or make its recommendation to an individual so charged. Further, the group may decide by majority rating or may be charged with reaching consensus.

Overall then, treatment analysis should be a systematic attempt to identify competing strategies, to assess them for their responsiveness to the needs data, and, for fit and appropriateness within the existing institution. Moreover, treatment analysis should be conducted so as to result in an implementation plan. Let us now return to the example to illustrate the treatment analysis.

To launch their effort, the evaluators and director of elementary education decided to use the advocacy team technique to stimulate the development of creative alternatives for responding to the situation in their district and community. As a first step in identifying advocacy positions and selecting team members, the district evaluator and the director of elementary education met with each school's PTA study team. Each team reported its own findings and recommendations regarding problems in its school. In the discussions that followed these reports, certain advocacy positions emerged. The people from Brown Elementary urged that a busing program be instituted. Members of the Henry group strongly recommended that their principal be replaced. The Smith team argued that they had worked hard to reach their present level of achievement and did not want their children from disadvantaged homes bused to another school or their staff members reassigned in other buildings. In effect, they argued in favor of the neighborhood school concept. The groups from Hays, Jones, and Foster asked for increased resources, but otherwise thought things should stay pretty much the same. Based on these discussions, the context information, and the superintendent's directive, two advocacy teams were formed; one for curriculum improvement through desegregation, and the other for curriculum improvement through neighborhood schools.

The teams were released from their other duties for one week and charged to develop and write their plans. They were instructed to show how the implementation of their plan would respond to the superintendent's directive and the problems identified by the previous district-wide and individual school studies. They were also told that their plans would be judged by the district evaluator for their potential effectiveness, fit with the existing curriculum, cost and general feasibility, innovativeness, legality, political viability, and fundablity.

When the two reports were submitted, it was clear that there was no winner (see table 4-6). The district evaluator and director of elementary education met with the two teams and superintendent to discuss the results and to form the convergence team. This team was composed of members of the two teams, an outside expert on integration, and one on elementary education. This team met for one week to prepare a plan. The resulting plan incorporated the two prior plans but added a magnet school dimension. Brown Elementary was proposed as a magnet school, to exemplify the philosophy that all children had gifts and talents and to provide a wide array of experiences in the creative and performing arts in addition to a sound basic education curriculum. Henry was designated as a magnet school to emphasize the philosophy of basic education. The Hays, Smith, and Foster Schools were to be retained as neighborhood schools and given additional funds to strengthen their programs. The hardest recommendation to make was that Jones School should be closed to insure integration and reduce administrative costs. To the extent possible, students were to be given their choice of the school they would attend, provided that this would result in each school having no more than 30 percent and no fewer

Table 4-6. Assessment of Alternative Advocacy Team Plans for Upgrading Elementary Education in the Black River School District

| | Plan 1: Busing Students and Redistribution of Teachers and Services | Plan 2: Upgrading Education in the Existing Neighborhood Schools |
|---|---|---|
| 1. Potential to upgrade the overall performance of Brown and Henry Schools | Strong | Weak |
| 2. Potential to preserve and strengthen performance in the other schools | Weak | Strong |
| 3. Potential to improve equality of educational opportunities | Strong | Weak |
| 4. Potential to integrate children of all socio-economic levels | Strong | Weak |
| 5. Provision for involving district personnel in the improvement program | Acceptable | Acceptable |
| 6. Overall potential effectiveness | Weak | Doubtful |
| 7. Fit with existing program | Weak | Strong |
| 8. Costs and general feasibility | Weak | Strong |
| 9. Innovativeness | Weak | Weak |
| 10. Legality | Strong | Weak |
| 11. Political viability | Weak | Weak |
| 12. Fundability | Doubtful | Weak |

than 10 percent of their students from underprivileged homes. Buses were to be provided for those students choosing magnet schools not within walking distance of their homes.

The evaluator prepared his final report, reflected in table 4-7, and submitted it to the superintendent. After discussing it with several school groups, he submitted the report to the board of education, along with his

Table 4-7. Assessment of Alternative Advocacy Team and Convergence Team Plans for Upgrading Elementary Education in the Black River School District

|  | *Plan 1:* *Busing* *Students and* *Redistribution* *of Teachers* *and Services* | *Plan 2:* *Upgrading* *Education* *in the* *Existing* *Neighborhood* *Schools* | *Plan 3:* *Combination* *of Magnet* *and* *Neighborhood* *Schools* |
|---|---|---|---|
| 1. Potential to upgrade the overall perform- ance of Brown and Henry Schools | Strong | Weak | Strong |
| 2. Potential to preserve and strengthen per- formance in the other schools | Weak | Strong | Strong |
| 3. Potential to improve equality of educa- tional opportunities | Strong | Weak | Strong |
| 4. Potential to integrate children of all socio- economic levels | Strong | Weak | Strong |
| 5. Provision for involving district personnel in the improvement program | Acceptable | Acceptable | Acceptable |
| 6. Overall potential effectiveness | Weak | Doubtful | Strong |
| 7. Fit with existing program | Weak | Strong | Strong |
| 8. Costs and general feasibility | Weak | Strong | Acceptable |
| 9. Innovativeness | Weak | Weak | Strong |
| 10. Legality | Strong | Weak | Strong |
| 11. Political viability | Weak | Weak | Doubtful |
| 12. Fundability | Doubtful | Weak | Strong |

recommendation that a modified version of the convergence team strategy be adopted. His modification was that Jones School should be open during the first year of the program and subsequently be closed only if the district-wide integration standard was not met during the first year. The board approved the recommendation and charged the superintendent to investigate how the plan could be funded.

We will leave this story here because it has served its purpose of illustrating the topics of this chapter. It should be noted, however, that needs analysis, strengths analysis, and treatment analysis lead only to the point of the adoption of an action plan. More evaluative work obviously would be required to guide the implementation of the program, to assess its effects, to examine its costs, and to conduct an ongoing assessment of needs and strengths in the program. It must not be assumed that implementation of the selected plan will automatically result in needs reduction. This is a question to be tested empirically. If the results are negative, recycling will be in order to repeat the needs assessment and search for a more effective strategy.

## Summary

In this chapter, the complex issue of analyzing data generated during the course of a needs assessment has been explored. It has been shown that analysis is not a one-time activity, but an ongoing iterative process with the results of one analysis and reactions to that analysis pointing the way to additional analyses. It has been argued that the analysis of needs assessment data should focus on student needs, program deficiencies and strengths, and solution strategies. Needs assessments are not decision-making procedures, but rather provide relevant information for the decision-making process. Often those doing the needs assessment are not the same people as those who must make the final decision. Thus, the next chapter addresses how to report needs assessment information in the most effective manner so that its potential utilization is maximized.

# 5 REPORTING NEEDS ASSESSMENT INFORMATION

This chapter presents practical guidelines and considerations for reporting needs assessment activities, results, and implications. It is divided into six major sections: (1) general guidelines; (2) functional elements in reporting; (3) preparing a reporting plan; (4) criteria for reporting; (5) reporting examples; and (6) charts, graphs, and tables.

The general purpose of reporting is communication. In the case of needs assessment, the purpose is either to inform an audience about the needs assessment or to enable them to make use of information from the needs assessment. In either case, it is crucial to effective reporting that neither the means nor the content of needs assessment communications be too narrowly defined. That is, reporting is *not* a static, one-time event nor is it necessarily a product such as a written report. Rather, reporting should be constructed as an ongoing process of varying communication events (oral, visual, written, etc.) that may start before the needs assessment begins and will likely continue beyond its conclusion. The content of reporting is not limited to communicating the findings of the needs assessment, but also includes communicating information about its purposes, context, means, results, and implications.

147

## General Guidelines

Perhaps the single most important guideline for the needs assessor to bear in mind is that reporting is intended to be a *communicative* process. Thus, those guidelines that bear on good communications in general will apply. Some important aspects of good communications are simplicity, clarity, directness, and confirmation/feedback.

*Keep it simple.* Reports should not be overly complex nor employ references and language not readily understood by their intended audiences. Education, as most professions, has a regrettable tendency to use jargon and complex language in presenting and transmitting ideas. Needs assessors should take extra care to use simple language, brief examples, and common expressions and terminology. For example, rather than say "The children display tendencies toward frequent aggressive and disruptive hostility and often emit acting-out behaviors in the presence of authority figures," one can state more simply, "The children often exhibit discipline problems." Technical language and jargon should be minimized at the very least and avoided if possible.

*Be clear.* Reports should be prepared and delivered without ambiguity. Needs assessments results often have multiple interpretations and are seldom precise and definite. Care must be taken, then, to insure that the report does not add further ambiguity. Findings should be clearly and simply presented and, where appropriate, alternative interpretations clearly listed and explained. Opinions and other subjective expressions should be clearly defined as such.

*Be direct.* Reports should directly address the purposes for which they are intended. This means the reporter should not ramble nor beat around the bush, but should focus on the major, salient points. An audience's time should be viewed as precious and, therefore, should not be wasted. This often means eliminating unnecessary content, providing only what is required for the consumer to receive and understand the intended communication.

*Provide for confirmation/feedback.* Good communication requires that people receiving messages be allowed to confirm their perceptions and understanding. Too often, as is true in interpersonal communications, messages received are quite different from messages sent or intended to be sent. When dialogue is possible, as in presentations or oral reports, provision for questions and discussion can meet these needs. For written or public media reports, provisions should be made for the audiences to check their understanding and interpretation of the content of the report through summaries, reviews, etc.

**Reporting Criteria**

The work of the Joint Committee on Standards for Educational Evaluations (1981) is especially applicable to needs assessment reporting. The criteria listed and explained below are derived directly from this work. As the Joint Committee has indicated, these standards are intended to serve a guiding function and are often in conflict with one another, thereby requiring trade-offs and balancing in their application to a given evaluation effort. The standards listed here are extracted and modified from those the Joint Committee believed were most applicable to the reporting function. Not *all* the standards that might apply to reporting are presented, nor is any one of those listed described in its entirety.

1. *Audience identification.* Audiences involved in or affected by the [needs assessment]* should be identified, so that their needs can be addressed.
2. *Information scope and selection.* Information collected should be of such scope and selected in such ways as to address pertinent questions about the object of the needs assessment and be responsive to the needs and interests of specified audiences.
3. *Valuational interpretation.* The perspectives, procedures, and rationale used to interpret the findings should be carefully described, so that the bases for value judgments are clear.
4. *Report clarity.* The needs assessment report should describe the object being evaluated and its context, and the purposes, procedures, and findings of the needs assessment, so that the audiences will readily understand what was done, why it was done, what information was obtained, what conclusions were drawn, and what recommendations were made.
5. *Report dissemination.* Needs assessment findings should be disseminated to clients and other right-to-know audiences, so that they can assess and use the findings.

---

*The term bracketed [needs assessment] replaces the term *evaluation* in the original text. For ease of reading, in the remainder of the listing, the brackets are deleted, although the term *needs assessment* has been substituted wherever *evaluation* appears.

6. *Report timeliness.* Release of reports should be timely, so that audiences can best use the reported information.

7. *Needs assessment impact.* Needs assessment should be planned and conducted in ways that encourage follow-through by members of the audiences.

8. *Full and frank disclosure.* Oral and written needs assessment reports should be open, direct, and honest in their disclosure of pertinent findings, including the limitations of the needs assessment.

9. *Public's right to know.* The formal parties to needs assessment should respect and assure the public's right to know, within the limits of other related principles and statutes, such as those dealing with public safety and the right to privacy.

10. *Rights of human subjects.* Needs assessments should be designed and conducted so that the rights and welfare of the human subjects are respected and protected.

11. *Balanced reporting.* The needs assessment should be complete and fair in its presentation of strengths and weaknesses of the object under investigation, so that strengths can be built upon the problem areas addressed.

12. *Object identification.* The object of the needs assessment (program, project, material) should be sufficiently examined, so that the form(s) of the object being considered in the needs assessment can be clearly identified.

13. *Context analysis.* The context in which the program, project, or material exists should be examined in enough detail so that its likely influences on the object can be identified.

14. *Described purposes and procedures.* The purposes and procedures of the needs assessment should be monitored and described in enough detail so that they can be identified and assessed.

15. *Defensible information sources.* The sources of information should be described in enough detail so that the adequacy of the information can be assessed.

16. *Justified conclusions.* The conclusions reached in a needs assessment should be explictly justified, so that the audiences can assess them.

17. *Objective reporting.* The needs assessment procedures should provide safeguards to protect the needs assessment findings and reports against distortion by the personal feelings and biases of any party to the needs assessment.

## Preparing a Reporting Plan

A reporting plan will show, in essence, who is to get the various reports, and why, when, and how. Decisions about this plan revolve around four reporting elements: purpose, audience, content, and format. Each of these elements bears on, and is a part of, the overall reporting plan. The planning process should begin with a determination of the purposes and audiences for the reporting function. In a sense, two interrelated elements represent the goals of the reporting function and thereby should precede the planning of the reporting content and formats.

The purposes for reporting should, of course, reflect and be compatible with the general purposes of the entire needs assessment effort. One must review, then, for whom the needs assessment is to be conducted and for what purposes. In consideration of these guiding purposes, the reporter should define the specific purposes the reporting is intended to address and the audiences that will suit those purposes. This can be done in a matrix format showing each purpose as it relates to different audiences. Such a matrix is provided in table 5-1. This general analysis of reporting needs and relevant audiences should be accompanied by considerable interaction with key members of each audience. That is, efforts must be made to determine the information needs perceived by each audience. This includes analyses of relevant guidelines, legislation, and mandate documents to determine minimal reporting requirements. The matrix display summarizes these efforts by showing who is to receive the reports and for what purposes.

The next planning step involves identifying the reporting events (such as written reports, meetings, presentations) necessary to fulfill the identified purposes for each audience. This work should culminate in a report *schedule* detailing each reporting event in terms of its intended content, format, audience, data, frequency, and so on. Such a report schedule is shown in table 5-2.

Getting reports to audiences when they are most likely to be needed, noticed, and important is crucial in getting them used. A report schedule should be both reactive and proactive. It must, of course, be responsive to the key planned events (for example, a board meeting) and opportunities where it may be useful. The schedule should also seek to issue reports that will be pertinent and timely for stimulating needed actions. In this respect, an interim report might be planned to occur before a conference or meeting

Table 5-1. Report Audiences

| Report Purposes | General Public | School Board | Needs Assessment Staff | District Administration | State Education Agency | Advisory Committee |
|---|---|---|---|---|---|---|
| Present needs assessment plans, purposes, general design | X | X | | X | | X |
| Provide accountability information regarding costs and progress of study | | | | X | X | |
| Information about progress and interim accomplishments | | X | X | X | | X |
| Present conclusions and findings | X | X | | X | X | X |

Table 5-2. Report Schedule

| Event | Date/Frequency | Format | Nature/Scope of Content | Audience |
|---|---|---|---|---|
| Monthly progress updates | End of month | Memorandum | Work accomplished, projected; problems, revisions to design; important future events | Needs assessment staff |
| Preliminary news release | 1st month of study | News story | Purpose, budget, organization, schedule, staff involved | General public |
| Interim media report | Near end of study after all data collected | Television interview with needs assessment director | Progress, preliminary findings, next steps, possible consequences | General public |
| Quarterly report | End of each quarter (90 days) | Written report | Progress, resources consumed, problems encountered, next step, revisions to plan | School board, administration, advisory committee |
| Final report: summary version | 30 days after end of study | Written report with no appendixes | Review of study, present data, conclusions, interpretations, recommendations | School board, administration advisory committee, others |
| Final report: technical | 90 days after end of study | Written report with appendixes (instruments, ect.) | Same as above, with fuller data reports included | Administration, SEA |
| Final report: hearing | 90 days after end of study | Panel review and public hearings with audio/visual presentation by needs assessment director | Data summaries, conclusion summaries, recommendations, implications | General public, school staff |

153

so that the subsequent event will be obligated to incorporate the report's content.

When you report to your intended audiences is not truly optional. Your schedule is pretty well fixed by your purposes. If a purpose is, for example, to help administrators decide whether to initiate a workshop series, they'll need your report just before they make the decision. But, you still need to consider how long before, and how often you should report. Here are some strategies that can be used to schedule report events:

1. Determine a report schedule based on events involving decision-making by the major audience. This entails scheduling reports to coincide with or immediately precede events such as the following:
   a. Board meetings
   b. Formal reviews and hearings
   c. Internal decision sessions (such as staff meetings)
   d. Public hearings
   e. Elections and referendums
   f. Budget determination hearings or meetings
   g. Caucuses
2. Schedule reports based on major events in the life of the system or programs of which the needs assessment is a part.
   a. Initiation of projects
   b. Completion of pilot workshops, trial classes, etc.
   c. Completion of phases (semesters, sessions, etc.)
   d. Completion of projects
3. Schedule according to commonly accepted time intervals:
   a. quarterly, semiannual, biannual, annual, etc.
   b. semesters, quarters
   c. fiscal years
4. Schedule reports by major events in the course of the needs assessment:
   a. Completion of the design
   b. Draft of tentative purposes and criteria
   c. Completion of preliminary analyses
   d. Signing of contract
   e. End-of-year report
5. Schedule opportunistically:
   a. Major problems discovered
   b. Delays in schedule
   c. Early success, rare occurrences
   d. Unexpected findings

    e. Ad hoc meetings, councils, boards, etc.
6. Schedule incrementally:
    a. News release, followed by
    b. Draft report for edit and review, followed by
    c. Preliminary report, followed by
    d. Final report, followed by
    e. Hearings and public discussion of results


Although there is an emphasis on planning implicit in our discussion thus far, the reader should not assume that preplanned reports are the *only* communications about the progress and results of the needs assessment that should occur. Opportunities and needs for additional reporting may occur, and when appropriate such reporting should be provided. The plan represents the minimal intended report schedule necessary for properly identifying the human, material, and financial resources required for the needs assessment. A formal plan also allows for an assessment of adequacy. That is, the report schedule can be evaluated to determine whether there is sufficient reporting to meet the identified purposes and if the plan is feasible, given the resources for the assessment.

## Functional Elements in Reporting

The four functional elements of reporting are:

1. Purpose: *Why* report the information?
2. Audience: *Who* will get the information?
3. Content: *What* information will they get?
4. Format: *How* will they get the information?

Although each of these elements is distinct, their interrelationship is the key to effective reporting. Each element gains its legitimacy from the other, and each must be appropriate in relation to the others to achieve effective communication.

### Purpose

The purposes of reporting were earlier identified as providing information to audiences about the needs assessment and enabling them to make use of information from the needs assessment. A critical precondition for designing and completing a reporting activity entails specifically delineating components of each of these generally stated purposes. Obviously, the content and format of a report are largely determined by just *why* there is to be a report in the first place. Within the general category of providing information, several purposes, or combinations of purposes, could be intended. Some of these are:

1. Accountability—denoting the needs that are being addressed, demonstrating how resources are being expended, what activities are taking place, who is involved, etc.
2. Education—enlightening the audience as to needs assessment purposes, procedures, problems, uses, etc.
3. Exploration—providing rationale for designs, purposes, problems, successes, failures, etc.
4. Involvement—attempting to draw uninvolved people and resources into the needs assessment.
5. Public relations—demonstrating the positive intentions and activities of the district or agency.
6. Gaining support—demonstrating the worth of the needs assessment and soliciting commitment and involvement.
7. Understanding—providing information that can be used to interpret information from the needs assessment.

Within the general intent of enabling audiences to utilize the needs assessment information, some usual purposes may be to design new programs; revise existing programs; reallocate resources; revise or conduct further needs assessments; determine other reporting activities; prioritize pupil needs; prioritize, select, or evaluate program (or treatment) alternatives; and make staffing, scheduling, or other administrative decisions.

### Audiences

Successful achievement of purpose is dependent upon the right audience receiving the information. Just as one must consider myriad purposes for reporting, it is useful to consider a broad range of potential audiences. The following list illustrates some of the audiences that may be considered.

Funding agencies                     PTA
Policy boards                        Licensing agencies

Program administrators        Legislators
Program staff                 Boards of education
Community organizations       Deans' offices
Parents                       Consumer groups
Pupils                        Department faculty
Community leaders             Department chairpersons
Teachers                      Curriculum committees
Consumers                     Boards of trustees
Advisory boards               Professional groups

The reporter must also be aware of various characteristics of the audiences, such as age, sex, occupation, educational background, level of experience, biases, motivational state, and familiarity with and knowledge of the content area to determine the appropriate terminology, setting, format, and content of the message to be conveyed.

Keep in mind that the greater the extent to which audiences are involved in the needs assessment, the more likely they are to use its results. Ideally, audiences will have been involved throughout the design and implementation of the needs assessment. This involvement should be continued in the planning and delivery of reports.

When considering which audiences are involved, it is best to differentiate them by the purposes for reporting to them; that is, not everyone should be reported to about everything. People should be given what they need and what is most responsive to their particular interests. Parents, for example, are less likely to want or need detailed information about how the study was conducted than they will need and want information about results.

The question of who should get what reports should be reviewed at different times during the life of the needs assessment. Changes in the needs assessment (for example, a new procedure, an unexpected finding) may indicate new audiences. Likewise, salient external events (such as a new grant in the district, the formation of a special interest group) may change or add to the audiences originally identified.

Once you are clear about just who should receive what reports, here are some tactics to generate audience involvement before and after reports are released:

1. Discuss the reports with key audience members.
2. Make oral presentations of the report.
3. Submit a rough draft of a report to some audience members for editing and a critique.
4. Distribute preliminary summary reports.

5.  Have audience members make their own reports, write reviews of the report, conduct meetings about the report, and so forth.
6.  Conduct panel meetings, hearings, and open forums on the report.
7.  Incorporate reports into training workshops in which audience members are involved.
8.  Present reports at professional associations and meetings.
9.  Invite commentary and reaction through publishing report summaries in journals and newsletters.
10. Attend meetings where reports can, but otherwise may not, be used and discussed.
11. Commission reviews, supportive papers, or other critiques and commentaries by people influential with key audiences.
12. Present reports at faculty meetings.
13. Conduct a conference around a report (for example, invite past graduates, some employers, and other faculty to a one-day conference on your study of needs, based on a survey of graduates.
14. Solicit questions, concerns, and related issues (using mail-back forms, 3 × 5 cards, etc.), following the release of a report.

*Content*

The content of the reports derives quite obviously from the process and findings of the needs assessment. The other major determinant of a report's content is its purpose. Content from the needs assessment that serves the purpose either directly or in a secondary, augmentative manner ought to be included. Content not relevant to the purpose should be excluded. The adverse consequences of including irrelevant content are far greater in a verbal reporting format than they are in a written format. In an oral presentation, for example, the listener cannot pick and choose from a table of contents those bits of the report most suitable to his or her needs. Audiences exposed to irrelevant content are likely to tune out some of the report, perhaps with more damaging consequences than if *no* report had been attempted.

The report may be more effectively received if it is preceded by an overview—an introductory summary in which the receiver is informed briefly about what is coming. This guideline derives from principles of education and communication. In order for readers or listeners to properly assimilate and comprehend a report's content, they require a cognitive organizer: a view of the "whole picture," into which the communication to follow is intended to fit. This front-end overview is a courtesy to an audience because it tells them what is coming and lets them choose to participate based on this information. More than courtesy, however, an overview makes good sense. The report should close with a summary. This reminds readers or participants of the report's main features and may suggest next steps or provide a basis for interaction.

Written reports, if properly organized, can enable a variety of audiences to select from the contents the information they need for a number of different purposes. A typical structure might include:

1. Précis or abstract—provides an overview of a report's content and allows a reader to decide if further reading is warranted.
2. Table of contents or other guide to organization—clearly labels portions of the report and indicates where they are located or how to gain access to them.
3. Introduction—relates the purpose of the report, its intended audience, scope and coverage, limitations, and organization. When selection among report parts is intended, the structure of such parts and rules for selection should be clearly provided. A preface, acknowledgments, or disclaimer section may also be required in the introductory content.
4. Body of report—contains information clearly organized around functional aspects related to the report's purpose. A report intending to explain the methods of a needs assessment might well be organized in a method-by-method presentation. Report content may also be organized according to the chronological order of activities; functional or conceptual stages; purposes, goals, and/or objectives; methods of data collection; major conclusions or results; or organizational or administrative units completing different parts of the study.
5. Summary—briefly reviews and highlights the major aspects of the report, its conclusions, significance, etc. This section might also include devices for readers to check their understanding and interpretation of the report.
6. Closing—gives implications for further related work or reporting and any additional information necessary for audiences to place the report in a proper context and perspective relative both to past and future events. This section may also provide or reiterate guidance to the audience about how they might further understand, use, or benefit from the report.

These content guidelines are intended primarily for written reports; however, they apply to other report formats as well. A presentation to a

PTA group, for instance, might well follow essentially the same general structure. The summary might consist of a review and a question-and-answer session and the closing might entail some concluding or reflective remarks by the superintendent. In any case, the content/structure guidelines ought to be considered a guide and adjusted and adapted where appropriate to differing report formats.

## Format

Reports may be presented in a variety of formats and media. The task is to insure that the format is appropriate to the content, audience, and purpose of the communication. It is important to remember that the medium affects the message. A popular medium such as magazines, television, or radio can accomplish broad dissemination, for example, but conveys a different aura than a journal article or a technical report. Likewise, the level of language (complexity, jargon, etc.) conveys messages in addition to its face value and, in any case, must be appropriate to intended audiences. Some formats for needs assessment reporting are:

Written documents: technical reports, interim and progress reports, conference proceedings

Media releases: print, television, radio

Meetings and small groups discussions, presentations

Hearings, panel reviews

Direct mail leaflets, pamphlets, newsletters

Staged interviews of key needs assessment participants, with a dissemination provision (television or radio coverage, transcripts)

Memoranda, letters, bulletins

Professional journals, other professional publications

Slide-tape, videotape, multimedia presentations

Mock jury "trials," socio-dramas, theatre

A key to selecting an effective format involves more than selecting an approach most likely to engage, interest, and involve the intended audience. As was stated earlier in this chapter, the evaluation information is most useful when it is shared in an interactive dialogue; one should therefore seek first those formats that allow for interaction between the reporter and the audience.

Another key guideline involves using varied techniques of presentation within any format. This not only incorporates more dynamism and intrinsic interest, but enables content to be reported and recombined without apparent redundancy, thereby enhancing understanding. Just as learning is more effective when it involves multiple senses, reporting can be more effective when it incorporates multiple format techniques. Thus, an oral presentation might be accompanied with written handouts, audiovisual aids, question-answer sessions, roleplays, etc. Care should be taken, of course, to avoid unnecessary redundancy or belaboring obvious messages. In sum, the means of reporting must be appropriate not only to audiences and purposes, but also to its content.

## Reporting Activities

As was noted earlier, reports may focus not solely on needs assessment results and conclusions, but also on conditions affecting the needs assessment: procedures, resources, design, interim results, problems encountered, and so forth. Virtually any aspect of the needs assessment process may require some type of reporting activity. Because a variety of reporting activities are frequently encountered during a needs assessment, a categorical list follows with a brief description of the content and/or purpose of each.

*Main needs assessment report.* Provides a comprehensive summary of the purposes, procedures, results, conclusions, and evaluation of the needs assessment.

*Technical report.* Includes a description of the information-gathering and analysis procedures and a detailed explanation of the information collected and analyzed.

*Appendixes.* Provide supplementary information to reports and consist of items such as copies of instruments, position papers, letters, previous reports.

*Interim reports.* Serve to document and communicate the progress of various needs assessment activities such as completion of the contract to conduct the study, agreement on the final design, collection and assembly of the basic information, completion of the preliminary analysis.

*Meetings and other interactive activities.* Events scheduled to coincide with the delivery of main and interim reports to enable audiences to explore and understand the content of the report.

*Informal reports.* Intended to augment and support formal reports of the study and may include activities such as a press conference to announce a contract agreement or present findings, an update memorandum to the school board, an article in the newspaper about participants in the study, a guest appearance by key personnel on a local television program, or other events and document releases that would serve to enhance understanding of and support for the needs assessment. Informal reports can be scheduled in the design of the needs assessment (as in chapter 2) or may be spontaneous as problems or events of special interest emerge.

*Internal reports.* Reports, not intended for external dissemination, that are used by the needs assessors as they conduct the study to facilitate decisions and progress at key points in the needs assessment process and to document key aspects of the assessment so that it can be evaluated and analyzed. In the example needs assessment design included at the close of chapter 2, several such reports were noted. These included a review of literature that helped the needs assessors identify relevant variables for data collection, a summary report of pupil test scores, site visit reports, and so forth. Internal reports are the working documents of the study. They may be included as appendixes in other reports or be cited in other reports as suitable.

## Reporting Examples

Following are a few brief examples of needs assessment reports in outline form. These are based on the example needs assessment presented in chapter 4, labeled according to report type (main, technical, interim, informal, or internal), and presented in chronological order.

In the example, a PTA group, school board, and superintendent had cooperated to conduct a study in relation to six elementary schools in their district, collecting ten kinds of information about student performance in each school along with other contextual information. During the preparation stage, the school district may well have issued one or more reports to inform the public and school personnel about the planned study. One of these would be a general press release announcing:

1. The reasons for and purposes of the needs assessment
2. The goals and objectives of the study
3. The groups (PTA, school board) and others involved (superintendent, district evaluator)
4. Some of the crucial issues involved (such as the desegregation order, socioeconomic variation among the schools)
5. The organization of the study (the five subgroups, steering committee)
6. The variables to be investigated and the general information methods to be used
7. A time frame for the study, listing its major planned events and report schedule

Another report that may be issued during the preparation stage prior to the press release is a statement by school personnel announcing the study. This would include:

1. All the information in the press release (items 1–7)
2. A delineation of the roles to be played by school personnel
3. The duties and responsibilities of school staff in supporting the study
4. The kinds of changes that might result from the needs assessment

During the course of the needs assessment, at least one interim report would be produced and scheduled for dissemination upon the completion of a major portion of the study or at a predetermined time interval such as after six months or at the end of the first year. In our example, the interim report might have been scheduled to occur when all the information planned for each needs assessment question had been collected and the preliminary analysis was slated to begin. This interim report would likely be issued in several forms. For example, an official school district summary report developed for distribution to PTA officials, school board members, central office staff, and others (school principals, the funding agency, etc.) would include:

1. An introduction reviewing the major purposes, scope and goals of the study, and delineating the audiences and content for the report
2. The general design (as outlined in chapter 2)

3. Progress to date, noting what data were collected, what persons have been involved, what reports have been made, and what problems, if any, have been encountered
4. An outline of the work that remains and a plan for its accomplishment. Here the PTA group's for preliminary analysis could be reviewed, and their subgroup organization and meeting schedule explained.

An internal data summary report prepared for use by the PTA group in their preliminary analysis would be organized by the major information collection procedures (pupil tests, interviews, newspaper accounts, cumulative folder data, etc.), and would display the aggregated information in a form amenable to analysis. An interim press release intended to inform the public of the study's progress and next steps would parallel the summary report.

In the study discussed in chapter 4, several internal interim reports were produced by the evaluator and presented to the PTA group analysis committees. These reports summarized and analyzed the results of additional information collection procedures he had employed such as the Delphi study and the cumulative bar graph display of each school's performance on the ten variables. Any of these internal reports might have formed the basis for press and media reports or have been combined in summary form for release as a second main interim report. The number of such main interim reports would depend largely on the scope, duration, and cost of the needs assessment. Generally, as these factors are increased, so are the number of interim reports.

When the treatment analysis was concluded, the final needs assessment reports would be completed. The main report would cover the entire needs assessment and could be organized in the following manner.

*Main Report Outline*

I. Introduction
   A. Primary intent of document (for example, to examine the adequacy of educating services and performance in the six schools and recommend a strategy for improving educational opportunity and performance)
   B. Audience(s) for the document (the study team, PTA, board of education, administration, funders, etc.)

C. Basic definitions (for example, need, met needs, unmet needs, and needs assessment)

D. Criteria for a sound needs assessment (utility, feasibility, propriety, and accuracy)

E. Limitations and caveats (time and resource constraints that must be taken into account and special problems such as technical problems, limits of analysis, generalization variable, etc.)

F. Overview of document (indicating which sections are most appropriate for each segment of the audience for the design)

II. Basic Information

A. Background (description of the events and discussions that led to the decision to do the assessment)

B. Groups involved (PTA, superintendent, staff of the six schools, parents, etc.)

C. Substantive focus (further description of the six schools in terms of demographic variables, achievement levels, and special problems; characterization of the relevant program(s) in each)

D. Information collected (the ten variables, contexts of the six schools, etc.)

E. Uses that will be made of the information (a decision regarding restructuring of program in the magnet and neighboring schools)

III. General Plan

A. Objectives of the assessment (to investigate school performance in the ten variables, to identify probable causes of low performance, to identify standards for performance levels, to identify treatment alternatives, etc.)

B. Logical structure (specifications of basic definitions—the ten variables, the context factors, etc.)

C. General procedures (the main techniques employed, for example, the collection of data on the ten variables, the PTA subgroup structure, the Delphi study, etc.)

D. Reports (identification and brief descriptions of reports available)

E. General schedule (an overall calendar indicating when the various data collection and reporting activities took place and which groups were involved at what times)

IV. Results and Conclusions

The "answers" to the three questions: expected levels of performance, current performance levels, factors related to low performance (the Delphi results, performance standards, relative school performance, indicators of educational development, etc.). This section would include tables, charts and graphs similar to those in chapter 4, accompanied by narrative explanations.

V. Treatment Needs Recommendations
This would detail the results of the advocacy teams, the relative ratings and comparisons of the two resultant plans, the convergence team plan, and a rating of that plan's adequacy.

VI. Evaluation of the Needs Assessment
Summary assessment of the needs assessment as per its costs, utility, propriety, and accuracy and a summary of strengths, weaknesses, and limitations of the study.

VII. Next Steps (for example, the plan for implementing the selected program strategy and assessing ongoing needs and strengths)

VIII. Appendixes (data summaries, interim reports, etc.)

The technical report, intended to supplement the main report, might be structured as follows:

*Technical Report Outline*

I. Introduction
 A. Primary intent
 B. Audience
 C. Basic definitions
 D. Limitations and caveats

II. Questions and Information Collected
 A. Enumeration (for example, listing of the four major questions, the ten variables, the information sources in each of the six schools)
 B. Comparison to objectives (matrix showing how the information collected was used to relate to the objectives of the study)

III. Sampling Plan
 A. Definition of population (for example, the six schools, grade levels examined, contextual factors of each school)
 B. Sampling specifications (numbers and types of samples drawn, numbers within each sample, such as how variables were accessed at each of the sixth grade levels, the stratified random samples, etc.)
 C. Procedures (how each sample was drawn, by whom, when)

IV. Information Collection Plan
  A. Instruments and procedures (descriptions of tests administered, Delphi group membership, site visit plans, etc.)
  B. Comparison to information needs (a matrix, as per chapter 3, showing how instruments and procedures relate to particular needs assessment questions)
  C. Procedures implemented (a description of how each procedure was implemented, by whom, when, where, etc.)
 V. Information Processing
  A. Screening and cleaning procedures (for each procedure, how data were verified and screened, noting re-collection when it occurred)
  B. Aggregation and filing (description of how the data were reduced, filed, and made ready for analysis)
VI. Preliminary Analysis
  A. Preliminary analysis procedures (such as description of the subcommittees formed, concerns identified, questions addressed, comparisons made among schools on attendance data.)
  B. Preliminary analysis results (description of each conclusion reached—the trends identified, issues defined, etc.)
VII. Needs and Strengths Analysis
  A. Questions addressed
  B. Procedures (description for each information set of how analysis was performed, such as the Delphi ranking of the ten variables, computation of school scores for each variable.)
  C. Analysis results (displays—bar graphs, tables, figures—and accompanying discussion of the results of each analytic procedure)


  *Note*: For clarity of communication, depending on the number of analyses, this section might be reorganized to report analytic procedures *and* results for each information collection procedure, rather than grouping all procedures together and all results together.
VIII. Recommendations
  This would focus on the procedures and results of the advocacy and convergence teams and present both policy and procedural recommendations.
IX. Appendixes
  These would contain raw data summaries, the internal data reports,

and other documents and reports that support the technical report and would be needed to replicate the analysis.

Finally, the release of the final report would be accompanied by one or more public meetings intended to enhance the understanding and utility of the needs assessment. For our example, this might take the form of a special PTA meeting to which the public media would be invited. Basic information in the main report would be presented, followed by a question and discussion period designed to enhance understanding of the report, facilitate its application, and identify implications for further study or reporting. The agenda for such a meeting might be:

### Agenda

I. Introduction by the Superintendent (15 minutes)
   A. Purposes, scope, and general design for the needs assessment
   B. Major parties involved
   C. Overview of the agenda
II. Review of the Assessment by the Chairperson of the PTA Study Team (30 minutes)
   A. Objectives of the study
   B. Procedures (overhead transparency: matrix of objectives and procedures)
   C. Results of analysis (overhead transparencies of cumulative bar graphs, school comparisons, etc.)
   D. Conclusions of the study: overview of advocacy team procedures, and convergence team conclusions
   E. Evaluation summary of limitations and caveats of the needs assessment
III. Questions for Clarification, Led by Superintendent, PTA Study Team Chairperson and Evaluator (15 minutes)
   Questions pertaining to clarification are raised by the audience and answered by an appropriate respondent.
Break—for coffee and rolls (20 minutes)
IV. Panel Discussion Moderated by Superintendent (60 minutes)
   A. Panel reactions. Each panelist gives a 3–5 minute reaction to or interpretation of the needs assessment.
   B. Public reactions. Audience members address questions to panel.
V. Evaluation (5 minutes)
   Participants complete brief survey questionnaire to record reactions to

meeting, rate extent to which each understands the study and supports its conclusions, and note additional questions/issues.
VI. Closing (5 minutes)
Superintendent thanks people for participating and briefly gives an overview of the next steps of the process.

## Charts, Graphs, and Tables

As we mentioned earlier in this chapter, much of needs assessment reporting necessarily focuses on quantitative data and other possibly complex information, such as relationships among several variables, rates, trends, comparisons, and so forth. It is important that this information be conveyed as clearly and concisely as possible. Graphic devices, if properly used, can assist greatly in this task. Such devices can be used effectively to support oral presentations, news conferences, and other dynamic reporting formats, as well as being used in their more traditional roles of written reporting.

In this closing portion of the chapter, several general kinds of graphic devices are presented, along with a few notes regarding their use. Needs assessors are encouraged to review and consider using these techniques as well as others for reporting needs assessment information. A guideline to remember here is although pictures are worth a thousand words, the use of graphs and charts in oral or written reports should never stand alone, but should always be accompanied by explanatory text. Each graph, chart, or table should always be labeled and supplemented with a brief discussion of its meaning.

### Charts

Charts are intended to depict processes, elements, roles, or other parts of some larger entity and their organization or interdependencies. The organization chart in figure 5-1 shows the relationship among roles, offices, and responsibilities.

The LOGOS (Language for Optimizing Graphically Ordered Systems) network is often used for program planning and analysis. It is used to show relationships of functions within a system. Arrows leading into a box indicate inputs to that function; the arrows leading out from a box indicate outputs of that function. Figure 5-2 is an example of this type of chart.

The Needs Assessment Staff

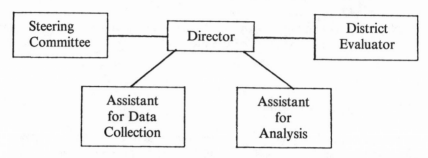

Figure 5-1.   Organization Chart.

Flow charts (fig. 5-3) are primarily used for planning and control, but can be used to report how a process works. Most flow charts make use of five symbols. An oval represents a starting and finishing space. Inputs and outputs are represented by parallelograms. Actions are shown by rectangles, and decisions are represented by diamond shapes. Arrows indicate the direction of flow.

The Information Collection Process

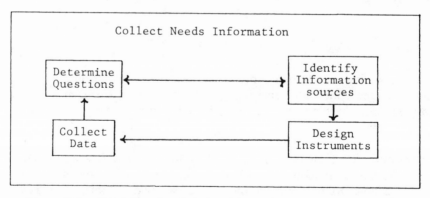

Figure 5-2.   Chart Showing Relationships of Functions Within a System.

Inservice Training Project

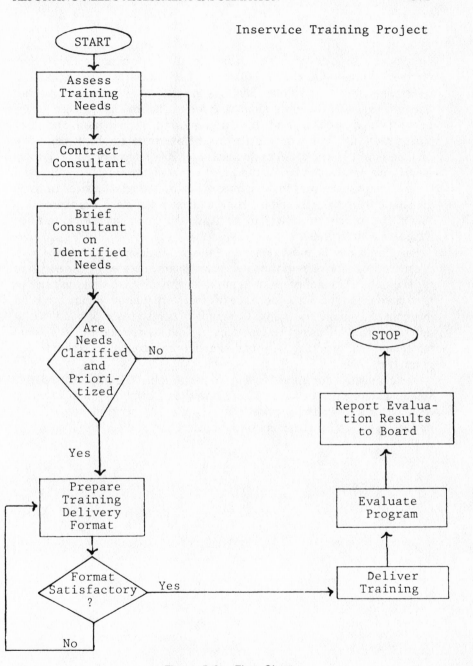

Figure 5-3.   Flow Chart.

*Graphs*

Graphs can be categorized according to the kind of information they represent. Three categories are summarized here: one-scale, two-scale, and a sampling of some variations. One-scale graphs contain information about only one variable. The most common types of one-scale graphs are the pie or circle graph, the area graph, the bar graph, and the pictogram. The pie or circle graph (fig. 5-4) is the simplest of the one-scale graphs. It can show only parts of the whole. All parts must total 100 percent or 360°. Two or more circle graphs can be used to provide a comparison.

Area graphs (fig. 5-5) make comparisons by the relative sizes of some geometric figures (for example, circle, square, rectangle. Since there is no "scale" by which amounts can be read, the exact quantities must be indicated with figure(s).

Bar graphs are the most versatile of the one-scale graphs. Relative sizes of the various categories of the single variable are indicated by the length of the line or bar. Greater precision is possible with this than with the circle or area charts, and there is less chance for misinterpretation. Figure 5-6 is an example of a simple bar graph. Comparison can be made of quantities at different times by using a second bar graph to provide the additional information or by adding information about the second time period to one graph (fig. 5-7).

The cumulative bar graph, seen in chapter 4, table 4-7, shows the relative standing among two or more units (schools) on a combination of variables (reading, math, health, physical fitness, etc.). The performance on *each* variable is shown by a segment of the vertical bar, and performance on the

Figure 5-4.  Circle Graphs. Actual District Inservice Training Expenditures.

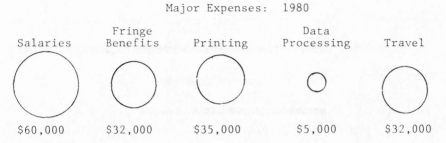

Figure 5-5. Area Graphs.

*sum* of the variables is shown by the cumulative height of the vertical bar.

The pictogram (fig. 5-8) is also a modification of the bar graph. Rather than using a line to represent quantity, figures are used. This is perhaps the most visually attractive graph, although it often sacrifices precision.

Two-scale graphs include the column (fig. 5-9) and line graphs. They can be used to show ordinal or interval data for two or more variables. The column graph appears to be a bar graph rotated 90 degrees, however, it contains two scales while the bar graph contains only one. Either graph can be horizontal or vertical, but usually the one-scale graph is better horizontally and the two-scale graph is better vertically.

The sliding graph (fig. 5-10) is a modification that can be made on either the column graph or the bar graph. This graph allows the presentation of negative quantities.

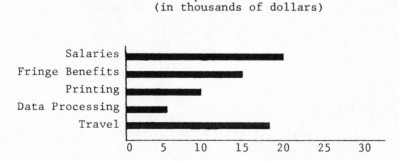

Figure 5-6. Simple Bar Graph. Expenses in 1979 (in thousands of dollars)

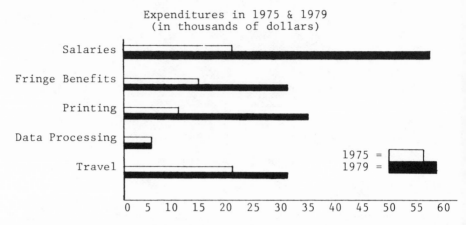

Figure 5-7. Bar Graph Comparing Data for Two Time Periods.

The line graph (fig. 5-11) can be used to convey the same types of information as the column graph, but the line graph is better when there are several points that must be plotted or where there are small changes between points. More lines may be plotted on the line graph to provide information for additional comparisons. Be careful not to provide too much information: four or five lines are usually the maximum.

The graphs illustrated and described here can be combined and varied in a number of ways. Full treatment of these variations is not possible here, but is described in Mary Spear's *Practical Charting Techniques* and in other

Expenditures in 1980

($ = $1,000)

|                  |   |   |   |   |   |   |   |
|------------------|---|---|---|---|---|---|---|
| Salaries         | $ | $ | $ | $ | $ | $ | $ |
| Fringe Benefits  | $ | $ |   |   |   |   |   |
| Printing         | $ | $ |   |   |   |   |   |
| Data Processing  | $ |   |   |   |   |   |   |
| Travel           | $ | $ | $ | $ |   |   |   |

Figure 5-8.  Pictogram. Expenditures in 1980 ($ = $1,000)

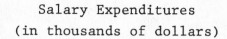

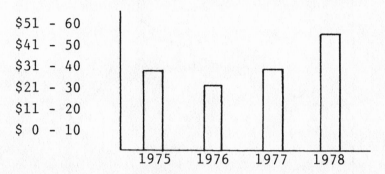

Figure 5-9. Column Graph. Salary Expenditures (in thousands of dollars)

Percentage of Projects Completed on Schedule

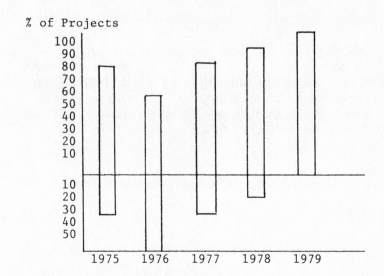

Figure 5-10. Sliding Graph.

Number of
Requests

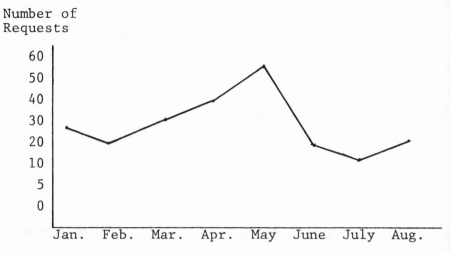

Figure 5-11. Line Graph. Resource Requests for January–August, 1979

publications. The ones illustrated and described here are but a small sample of possibilities.

### Tables

Tables present information in numerical form, words or phrases, or symbols in rows and columns arranged so that relationships and trends can be readily identified. They may be quite simple, showing single variables, or quite complex, showing multiple variables and depicting several interrelationships. The simple *one-way table* is illustrated by table 5-3.

Table 5-3.   One-Way Table: No. of Teachers in Detroit Schools

| Building | Total No. of Teachers |
|----------|-----------------------|
| A | 21 |
| B | 17 |
| C | 24 |
| D | 18 |

Table 5-4. Two-Way Table: Incidence of Crime in Schools (Annual Average)

| Socioeconomic Status of Schools | Type of Crime | | Total |
|---|---|---|---|
| | Minor | Major | |
| High | n = 73 | n = 4 | 77 |
| Low | n = 81 | n = 36 | 117 |
| Total | 154 | 40 | 194 |

The *two-way table* (table 5-4) is used to show the frequency (rate of occurrence, amount, etc.) of two variables and also to indicate the relationship (correlation) between the variables.

The *three-way table* (table 5-5) depicts one variable as it relates to two other variables. Because of their complexity, these tables generally require (except for audiences skilled in their use) a lot of textual support and explanation. These would be most often used in a technical report.

## Summary

Reporting needs assessment information has been discussed as an ongoing and key part of the whole needs assessment effort. It is the means by which needs data are made available and interpreted for decision-making. It was

Table 5-5. Three-Way Table: Participation in Inservice (Percent Acquiring Three Hours or More Per Year) for Teachers, by Schools, According to Tenure Status and Grade Level

| | Grades K–2 | | Grades 1–3 | | Grades 4–6 | |
|---|---|---|---|---|---|---|
| | Tenure (%) | No Tenure (%) | Tenure (%) | No Tenure (%) | Tenure (%) | No Tenure (%) |
| School A | 6 | 22 | 5 | 19 | 5 | 14 |
| School B | 23 | 74 | 18 | 60 | 14 | 53 |
| School C | 40 | 93 | 38 | 70 | 27 | 62 |

noted that reporting should adhere to the general principles of good communications: it should be concise, clear, use appropriate language for audiences, and employ effective means and formats. It is particularly important that reporting not be construed as a linear one-way event, but that reported information be seen as a stimulus around which discussion and interaction can occur to bring meaning, interpretation, and utility to needs assessments. Thus, reporting is often designed to include interaction between needs assessors and advisers through formats such as hearings, meetings, conferences, and presentations.

Four elements of reporting were defined: purpose, audience, content, and format. Consideration of these four elements is crucial to effective reporting, and each must be appropriate to the others. As there are several purposes to be served by reporting, so are there multiple audiences, content elements, and formats.

The preparation of a reporting plan and criteria for reporting were discussed and some reporting examples presented. The chapter closed with examples of some frequently used graphic devices, noting the kinds of information each can be used to communicate.

# 6 EVALUATING THE NEEDS ASSESSMENT

This final chapter is concerned with evaluating a needs assessment. Many things can and often do go wrong in needs assessments, and, accordingly, they should be checked for problems such as bias, technical error, administrative difficulties, and misuse. Such checks can be helpful for strengthening a needs assessment plan, managing the process, interpreting the findings, and promoting appropriate uses of the reports. In general, evaluations of needs assessments are helpful both to guide and improve the studies and to report publicly on their strengths and weaknesses. This chapter includes a discussion of the reasons for evaluating a needs assessment, standards and questions to guide evaluations of needs assessment, and some ways of doing the evaluations. Also included are pertinent checklists, charts, and forms.

## Why Evaluate a Needs Assessment?

Needs assessments provide a basis for decisions about which persons will receive what services and what goals will be pursued, and, of course, they consume valuable resources. It is important therefore to insure that they provide valid, useful information; that they are implemented efficiently; and

179

that they are properly used. One means of insuring the quality of needs assessments is to evaluate assessment plans, processes, and reports periodically. The following information can be obtained from such evaluations:

1. Clarification and assessment of the goals and procedural plan of the needs assessment
2. Detection of problems when implementing the needs assessment before it becomes too difficult or impossible to correct them
3. Documentation of the needs assessment process to assist in judging its end products
4. Assessment of the overall dependability of the needs assessment and its findings
5. Cost information that can help to reduce costs of future needs assessments
6. Assessment of the uses of the needs assessment
7. Feedback to help the needs assessors improve their assessment skills

More particular concerns that should be considered in evaluating the needs assessment are represented by the following questions:

1. Was the needs assessment study responsive to the audiences' questions?
2. Was the scope of the study sufficient and appropriate?
3. Were those involved in the needs assessment credible?
4. Was the needs assessment plan implemented appropriately?
5. Were needs assessment reports available when needed?
6. Were the reports given in a format useful to the audiences?
7. Were reports provided to all appropriate audiences?
8. Are the results accurate and unequivocal?
9. How internally consistent are the findings, and how consistent would they be under test-retest conditions?
10. Would competent judges agree with the findings or are the results highly dependent on the unique experience, biases, and interests of the needs assessors?
11. Were the conclusions of the study justified by the collected information?
12. Can the findings be applied to groups or settings not actually studied?
13. To what degree were the objectives of the needs assessment fulfilled?

14.  Does the needs assessment represent an improvement in practice or theory?
15.  What improvements in practice and theory are needed?

Although this list is not exhaustive, these questions illustrate the range of concerns about a needs assessment that should be investigated. The degree to which these questions apply to a given needs assessment will vary with the purpose and design of the assessment.

## Standards of a Good Needs Assessment

In addition to addressing questions such as those listed above, needs assessments should be judged against appropriate and generally agreed-upon standards. A national committee called the Joint Committee on Standards for Educational Evaluations has identified and defined 30 standards for use in assessing evaluations of educational programs, projects, and materials. We think these standards are also applicable to evaluations of needs. A general description of the standards is provided in this chapter; however, users should study the full text of the standards as presented in the Joint Committee's report (1981).

The standards are grouped according to four attributes of a study—utility, feasibility, propriety, and accuracy. In presenting the standards, we have substituted *needs assessment* for *evaluation* in all 30 of the standards.

### Utility

The utility standards reflect the general consensus that emerged in the educational evaluation literature during the late 1960s—that evaluators should address the information needs of their clients. In general, the utility standards require investigators to acquaint themselves with their audiences, to ascertain the audiences' questions, to obtain relevant information, to report it clearly and in a timely manner, and to help the audiences to use it.

The descriptors and definitions of the eight utility standards follow:

(A1)  *Audience identification.* Audiences involved in or affected by the needs assessment should be identified, so that their needs can be addressed.

(A2) *Evaluator credibility.* Those conducting the needs assessment should be both trustworthy and competent to perform the needs assessment, so that their findings achieve maximum credibility and acceptance.

(A3) *Information scope and selection.* Information collected should be of such scope and selected in such ways as to address pertinent questions about the object of the needs assessment and be responsive to the needs and interests of specified audiences.

(A4) *Valuational interpretation.* The perspectives, procedures, and rationale used to interpret the findings should be clearly described, so that the bases for value judgments are clear.

(A5) *Report clarity.* The needs assessment report should describe the group whose needs are being evaluated and its location, and the purposes, procedures, and findings of the needs assessment, so that the audiences will readily understand what was done, why it was done, what information was obtained, what conclusions were drawn, and what recommendations were made.

(A6) *Report dissemination.* Needs assessment findings should be disseminated to clients and other right-to-know audiences, so that they can assess and use the findings.

(A7) *Report-timeliness.* Release of reports should be timely, so that audiences can best use the reported information.

(A8) *Evaluation impact.* Needs assessments should be planned and conducted in ways that encourage follow-through by members of the audiences.

## Feasibility

The standards concerned with feasibility are consistent with the growing realization that evaluation procedures must be cost effective and workable in real world settings. These standards recognize that evaluations usually must be conducted in a dynamic social setting (as opposed to a contrived and controlled setting) and that they consume valuable resources. These standards require that the study plan be operable in the setting in which it is to be applied and that no more materials and personnel time than necessary be consumed. Overall the feasibility standards call for studies that are realistic, prudent, diplomatic, politically viable, and frugal.

The descriptors and definitions of the Joint Committee's three feasibility standards are as follows:

(B1) *Practical procedures.* The needs assessment procedures should be practical, so disruption is kept to a minimum and needed information can be obtained.

(B2)   *Political viability.* The needs assessment should be planned and conducted with an anticipation of the different positions of various interest groups, so that their cooperation may be obtained and also to avert or counteract possible attempts by any of these groups to curtail needs assessment operations or to bias or misapply the results.

(B3)   *Cost effectiveness.* The needs assessment should produce information of sufficient value to justify the resources expended.

## Propriety

The propriety standards reflect the fact that evaluative studies affect many people in various ways. These standards aim to insure that the rights of persons affected by a study will be protected. Taken as a whole, the propriety standards require that evaluations be conducted legally, ethically, and with due regard for the welfare of those involved in the study as well as those affected by the results.

The descriptors and definitions of the Joint Committee's eight propriety standards are as follows:

(C1)   *Formal obligation.* Obligations of the formal parties to a needs assessment (what is to be done, how, by whom, when) should be agreed to in writing, so that these parties are obligated to adhere to all conditions of the agreement or formally to renegotiate it.

(C2)   *Conflict of interest.* Conflict of interest, frequently unavoidable, should be dealt with openly and honestly, so that it does not compromise the needs assessment processes and results.

(C3)   *Full and frank disclosure.* Oral and written needs assessment reports should be open, direct, and honest in their disclosure of pertinent findings, including the limitations of the needs assessment.

(C4)   *Public's right to know.* The formal parties to a needs assessment should respect and insure the public's right to know, within the limits of other related principles and statutes, such as those dealing with public safety and the right to privacy.

(C5)   *Rights of human subjects.* Needs assessments should be designed and conducted, so that the rights and welfare of the human subjects are respected and protected.

(C6)    *Human interactions.* Needs assessors should respect human dignity and worth in their interactions with other persons associated with the needs assessment.

(C7)    *Balanced reporting.* The needs assessment should be complete and fair in its presentation of strengths and weaknesses of the program or group being studied so that its strengths can be built upon and its problem areas addressed.

(C8)    *Fiscal responsibility.* The evaluator's allocation and expenditure of resources should reflect  sound accountability procedures and otherwise be prudent and ethically responsible.

### Accuracy

The accuracy standards determine whether a study has produced sound information. These standards require that the obtained information be technically adequate and that conclusions are derived logically from the data. The overall rating of a study against the accuracy standards will provide a solid estimate or assessment of the overall validity of the needs assessment.

The descriptors and definitions of the eleven accuracy standards are the following:

(D1)    *Object identification.* The group whose needs are being assessed should be sufficiently examined so that it can be clearly identified and characterized.

(D2)    *Context analysis.* The context in which the group exists should be examined in enough detail so that its likely influences on the group can be identified.

(D3)    *Described purposes and procedures.* The purposes and procedures of the needs assessment should be monitored and described in enough detail that they can be identified and assessed.

(D4)    *Defensible information sources.* The sources of information should be described in enough detail that the adequacy of the information can be assessed.

(D5)    *Valid measurement.* The information-gathering instruments and procedures should be chosen or developed and then implemented in ways that will insure that the interpretation arrived at is valid for the given use.

(D6)    *Reliable measurement.* The information-gathering instruments and procedures should be chosen or developed and then implemented in ways that will insure that the information obtained is sufficiently reliable for the intended use.

(D7)   *Systematic data control.* The data collected, processed, and reported in a needs assessment should be reviewed and corrected, so that the results of the needs assessment will not be flawed.

(D8)   *Analysis of quantitative information.* Quantitative information in a needs assessment should be appropriately and systematically analyzed to insure supportable interpretations.

(D9)   *Analysis of qualitative information.* Qualitative information in a needs assessment should be appropriately and systematically analyzed to insure supportable interpretations.

(D10)  *Justified conclusions.* The conclusions reached in a needs assessment should be explicitly justified, so that the audiences can assess them.

(D11)  *Objective reporting.* The needs assessment procedures should provide safeguards to protect the needs assessment findings and reports against distortion by the personal feelings and biases of any party to the needs assessment.

## Use of the Standards

The Joint Committee standards may be used to serve two main roles: to plan and guide a needs assessment (a formative evaluation of the assessment); and to assess and publicly report its strengths and weaknesses (summative evaluation of the assessment). In the first of these roles, the standards can help the needs assessors and their client:

1. Decide whether to conduct a needs assessment
2. Identify and assess the purposes to be served
3. Assess and strengthen the political viability of the needs assessment
4. Reach and monitor contractual agreements that will govern the assessment
5. Staff the assessment
6. Develop plans for managing the assessment
7. Develop and administer data collection instruments
8. Analyze the obtained information (both quantitative and qualitative)
9. Report the findings
10. Use the results

These ten points are typical of the tasks that must be considered when designing and conducting a needs assessment and the standards are a potentially useful source of guidance for conducting these tasks. In general, all 30 of the standards should be applied to each task; however, some of them will typically be more useful than others, depending on the task.

Table 6-1 serves as a general guide for determining which standards should receive highest priority for each of the ten tasks listed above. The row headings are the descriptors, while the column headings are the tasks. This table can be used as a set of agendae for various meetings that pertain to planning and executing an assessment, as a guide to planning given needs assessment activities, and as a checklist for reviewing progress in an assessment. As may be inferred from the table, there is no consistent ordering of the standards in regard to importance or precedence. They are general principles that take on different degrees of usefulness depending on circumstances in a given study. Therefore, the standards must be applied flexibly and judiciously, and the needs assessors and their clients should keep in mind that using the standards as guidelines in the needs assessment will help insure that the studies will ultimately prove useful, feasible, proper, and technically sound.

The nature of this ultimate aim for a good needs assessment brings us to the second way in which the standards may be used. This is to assess the overall worth of the needs assessment. Typically, such summative evaluations are conducted after the needs assessment has been completed to help people decide whether they should trust and use the findings. However, such evaluations also may be done before or during an assessment (for example, to decide whether a study is hopelessly flawed and should therefore be stopped). In summative evaluations of needs assessments, all of the standards should be considered and judgments should be reported whether or not they come from people and groups with or without vested interest in promoting or attacking the study. On a constructive note, such summative evaluations of a needs assessment can help audiences make constructive use of findings, avoid misinterpretations, and guard against putting more confidence in findings than is warranted.

### Applying the Standards

Needs assessors who wish to use the Joint Committee's 30 standards in the ways identified above should become thoroughly familiar with the full text of the standards. They should reference the standards in their needs assessment designs and reports, acquaint their clients and their audiences

Table 6-1. Analysis of the Relative Importance of 30 Standards in Performing 10 Tasks in a Needs Assessment

| Standards (Descriptors) | (1) Deciding Whether to do a Study | (2) Clarifying and Assessing Purpose | (3) Endure Political Viability | (4) Contract | (5) Staff the Study | (6) Manage the Study | (7) Collect Data | (8) Analyze Data | (9) Report Findings | (10) Apply Results |
|---|---|---|---|---|---|---|---|---|---|---|
| A1 Audience Identification | X | X | X | X | | X | | | X | X |
| A2 Evaluator Credibility | X | | X | X | X | X | X | | | |
| A3 Information Scope and Selection | | | | X | | | X | | X | |
| A4 Valuational Interpretation | | X | X | | | | X | X | X | X |
| A5 Timely Reporting | | | | X | | X | | | X | |
| A6 Report Dissemination | | | X | X | | X | | | X | X |
| A7 Clear Reporting | | | | | | | | | X | |
| A8 Evaluation Impact | X | X | X | | | | | | X | X |
| B1 Practical Procedures | | | X | | | | X | X | | |
| B2 Political Viability | X | | X | X | X | X | X | | | X |
| B3 Cost Effectiveness | X | X | | | | X | | | | |
| C1 Formal Obligation | X | | X | X | | X | X | | | X |
| C2 Conflict of Interest | X | X | X | X | X | X | | | | X |
| C3 Full & Frank Disclosure | | | | | | | | | X | |

Table 6-1 (continued)

| Standards (Descriptors) | (1) Deciding Whether to do a Study | (2) Clarifying and Assessing Purpose | (3) Endure Political Viability | (4) Contract | (5) Staff the Study | (6) Manage the Study | (7) Collect Data | (8) Analyze Data | (9) Report Findings | (10) Apply Results |
|---|---|---|---|---|---|---|---|---|---|---|
| C4 Public's Right to Know | | | X | X | | | | | X | X |
| C5 Rights of Human Subjects | | | X | X | | X | X | | | X |
| C6 Human Interactions | | | X | | | X | X | | | |
| C7 Balanced Reporting | | | | | | X | X | | X | X |
| C8 Fiscal Responsibility | | | X | X | | X | | | | |

| | | | | | | | |
|---|---|---|---|---|---|---|---|
| D1 | Object Identification | X | X | | X | | X | X |
| D2 | Context Analysis | X | X | | X | | X | X |
| D3 | Described Purp. & Procd. | X | X | X | X | | X | X |
| D4 | Defensible Inf. Sources | X | | X | X | | X | |
| D5 | Valid Measurement | | | | X | | X | |
| D6 | Reliable Measurement | | | | X | | | |
| D7 | Systematic Data Control | | | X | X | | | |
| D8 | Quantitative Analysis | | | | | X | | |
| D9 | Qualitative Analysis | | X | | | X | | |
| D10 | Justified Conclusions | X | | | X | X | X | X |
| D11 | Objective Reporting | | | X | | X | X | X |

Table 6-2. Standard Criterion Form

The Standards for Evaluations of Educational Programs, Projects, and Materials guided the development of this (check one):

____ request for evaluation plan/design/proposal
____ evaluation plan/design/proposal
____ evaluation contract
____ evaluation report
____ other

To interpret the information provided on this form, the reader needs to refer to the full text of the standards as they appear in Joint Committee on Standards for Educational Evaluation, Standards for Evaluations of Educational Programs, Projects, and Materials, New York.

The Standards were consulted and used as indicated in the table below (check as appropriate):

| Descriptor | The Standard was deemed applicable and to the extent feasible was taken into account | The Standard was deemed applicable but was not taken into account | The Standard was not deemed applicable | Exception was taken to the Standard |
|---|---|---|---|---|
| A1 Audience Identification | | | | |
| A2 Evaluator Credibility | | | | |
| A3 Information Scope & Selection | | | | |
| A4 Valuational Interpretation | | | | |
| A5 Report Clarity | | | | |
| A6 Report Dissemination | | | | |
| A7 Report Timeliness | | | | |
| A8 Evaluation Impact | | | | |

190

B1   Practical Procedures

B2   Political Viability

B3   Cost Effectiveness

C1   Formal Obligation

C2   Conflict of Interest

C3   Full and Frank Disclosure

C4   Public's Right to Know

C5   Rights of Human Subjects

C6   Human Interactions

C7   Balanced Reporting

C8   Fiscal Responsibility

D1   Object Identification

D2   Context Analysis

D3   Described Purp. & Procedures

D4   Defensible Information Sources

D5   Valid Measurement

D6   Reliable Measurement

D7   Systematic Data Control

D8   Analysis of Quantitative Inf.

D9   Analysis of Qualitative Inf.

D10   Justified Conclusions

D11   Objective Reporting

Table 6-2. *(continued)*

Name: _____ Date: _____

       (typed)

_____

       (signature)

Position or Title: _____

Agency: _____

Address: _____

Relation to Document: _____

(e.g., author of document, evaluation team leader, external auditor, internal auditor) with the standards, use the standards as a basis for planning and guiding their studies and often should negotiate for independent evaluations of their needs assessments based on the standards. To aid users of the standards in deciding how they apply in a given situation and to communicate how they were used, the Joint Committee has developed a standards citation form. The Committee has granted general permission to reproduce this form, and a copy appears as table 6-2. As seen in the form, users of the standards are asked to decide which standards were judged applicable and taken into account, which ones were judged applicable but were not taken into account, which ones were deemed inapplicable, and which ones were judged wrong or inappropriate. By completing this form and appending it to needs assessment plans and reports, clients and audiences will be directed to the full text of the standards and thereby helped to judge the worth of plans and reports. This is viewed as a minimal service to the users of needs assessment studies, and it is hoped that needs assessors increasingly will make arrangements so that their audiences and clients also receive independent reports that evaluate the merits of given needs assessments. The Joint Committee's 30 standards comprise a set of principles that can undergird such evaluations. Minimally, a report that presents a summative evaluation of a needs assessment should include brief written assessments of the needs assessment for each of the 30 standards.

## Evaluation Questions

The evaluation standards discussed above are a major foundation of the professional practice of evaluation and should be considered when doing needs assessments. Another source of evaluation criteria and concerns would be questions that might be addressed to avoid problems that commonly affect needs assessments. A list of such questions appears in appendix 6A. There is considerable overlap with the stated and implied concerns from the evaluation standards. However, the list of questions reflects problems that are commonly encountered in evaluation work and in some circumstances may be a preferred form for identifying evaluation concerns.

Sanders and Nafziger (1975) offer a second set of questions regarding the adequacy of evaluation designs that can be used to assess needs assessment designs. These questions appear below in checklist format (appendix 6B), and can be used to assess the adequacy of a needs assessment design before implementation.

**Types of Evaluation**

The standards and lists of questions provide conceptual tools for evaluating needs assessments, but procedural plans are also needed.

*Assessment of a Needs Assessment Plan*

Before starting a needs assessment, its plan should be carefully examined. This involves evaluating the preparation phase and its resulting products, for example, design, contract, and management design. It also entails assessing the degree to which the appropriate groups had been adequately involved; the degree to which a clear direction and specific procedures have been chosen, the degree to which the needs assessment is likely to be implemented successfully, whether planning has been done in a comprehensive and exhaustive manner, etc. Evaluation of the preparation phase should help the needs assessors to confirm that the assessment should be done and to strengthen the plan.

One way to assess the preparation stage of a needs assessment is to conduct a structured group interview with the assessor, client, and representatives of the other audiences. In such an interview, primary emphasis should be on assuring that the projected needs assessment results would be worth the time, costs, and trouble required to obtain them. If not, a decision to terminate is in order. Assuming a decision to proceed, this group should systematically look for problems in their plans and ways to address them.

The agenda for the group interview might follow the 30 Joint Committee standards or either of the checklists previously introduced. The evaluators of the needs assessment should explain each standard or checkpoint, then probe with pertinent questions. They should draw out the participation of all members of the group to insure that all relevant problems and issues are uncovered. And they should solicit suggestions—sometimes decisions from those with the relevant authority—for dealing with the identified problems and issues. Minutes of the meeting should be kept, and the evaluators should subsequently present a report that describes the proceedings, critiques the needs assessment plan, and provides recommendations for improving the plan. This report might become the basis for a subsequent workshop aimed at revising the plan and/or orienting the person or group assigned to carry it out.

## Assessment of the Needs Assessment Process

Periodic checks should be made on how well the needs assessment is being implemented. Is the needs assessor on board and doing the job? Is the plan being carried out appropriately and on schedule? Are the data collection instruments sound, and is an adequate and appropriate amount of information being accumulated? Are sufficient resources being invested in the needs assessment? Are the relevant authority figures supporting the study appropriately? What communications are being issued, and are the audiences finding them of use? Should the needs assessment plan be revised? Are there any other problems? What kind of assistance does the needs assessment team need?

A group meeting might be used to assess the implementation of a needs assessment. Again, the Joint Committee's standards or an appropriate checklist of questions or potential problems could be used to guide the meeting. In addition, the evaluators should examine records, instruments, and data, and interview key participants and audiences. The evaluator should maintain notes on pertinent observations, feedback obtained from interviews, and judgments of information reviewed. Both oral and written reports should be submitted.

Sometimes a workshop should be conducted. It might begin with a review and discussion of the findings of the interim evaluation. The participants might next be asked to agree on ways to improve their needs assessment work. Then small groups could work on this agenda for a few hours. Small group reports could then provide a basis for further discussion. Finally, the participants might help the evaluator update the plans for further evaluations of the needs assessment.

## Summative Evaluation of a Needs Assessment

Summative evaluation addresses the question: How good and valuable was the needs assessment? In terms of the Joint Committee's standards, was it useful, practical, proper, and valid? Also, were the results used and were they used appropriately? For example, did the assessment lead to clearer and more defensible goals? If the needs assessment information was flawed, why? If the information was sound but was not used, why not? Obviously, a summative evaluation of a needs assessment must concentrate on determining the quality and impact of final reports; but it must also examine the appropriateness and quality of the data gathering and reporting processes. Therefore, the final evaluation of a needs assessment should integrate its findings with those produced in prior assessments of the needs assessment plan and process.

A final concern relates to the scope of the effort necessary to evaluate a needs assessment. This will vary with the cost, importance, and magnitude of the needs assessment. It may be done by the needs assessor, perhaps periodically using a simple checklist to rate the degree to which standards have been met. Or the evaluation may be done by a team of experts using extensive information-gathering and analysis procedures. Their reports might be both written and oral and could be presented and used in workshop settings.

Effective management of the needs assessment requires that an appropriate evaluation process occur. The evaluation standards, sample evaluation questions, and checklists supplied in this chapter, as well as the checklist in chapter 1, can be used to determine the concerns and criteria to guide the evaluation of a particular needs assessment. They can also be used to arrive at judgments of needs assessment plans, processes, and findings. Such evaluations are crucial because needs assessments are costly, can have major impact on people, and are currently an evolving set of procedures, practices, and concepts in need of improvement.

### Summary

This chapter has called attention to the value of evaluating needs assessments. Thirty standards that are potentially useful for judging needs assessments were presented, and recommendations were offered concerning appropriate uses of the standards. The standards can serve both as a list of concerns to be considered when planning an assessment and as a set of criteria for evaluating an assessment that has been completed. Likewise, two checklists of questions and potential problems were offered that can be used similarly to the standards. Evaluation of needs assessments is crucial to assure that they provide sound and effective guidance for improving education.

# APPENDIX 6A
# QUESTIONS FOR EVALUATING
# A NEEDS ASSESSMENT
## By: Daniel L. Stufflebeam

*Conceptualization of Needs Assessment*

____ Definition — How is needs assessment defined in this effort?

____ Purpose — What purpose(s) will it serve?

____ Questions — What questions will it address?

____ Information — What information is required?

____ Audiences — Who will be served?

____ Agents — Who will do it?

____ Process — How will they do it?

____ Standards — By what standards will their work be judged?

*Sociopolitical Factors*

____ Involvement — Whose sanction and support is required, and how will it be secured?

____ Internal communication — How will communication be maintained between the needs assessors, the sponsors, and the system personnel?

_____ Internal credibility     Will the needs assessment be fair to persons inside the system?

_____ External credibility     Will the needs assessment be free of bias?

_____ Security     What provisions will be made to maintain security of the information?

_____ Protocol     What communication channels will be used by the needs assessor and system personnel?

_____ Public relations     How will the public be kept informed about the intents and results of the needs assessment?

*Contractual/Legal Arrangements*

_____ Client/Needs assessor relationship     Who is the sponsor, who is the needs assessor, and how are they related to what is being studied?

_____ Needs assessment products     What are the intended outcomes of the needs assessment?

_____ Delivery schedule     What is the schedule of needs assessment activities and products?

_____ Editing     Who has the authority for editing reports?

_____ Access to the data     What existing data may the needs assessors use, and what new data may they obtain?

_____ Release of reports     Who will release the reports and what audiences may receive them?

_____ Responsibility and authority     Is it clear as to who is to do what in the needs assessment?

_____ Finances     Have the necessary resources been determined and is it clear how they will be provided?

*Technical Design*

_____ Objectives and variables     What is the needs assessment designed to achieve, in what terms should it be evaluated?

_____ Investigatory framework     Under what conditions will the information be gathered, for example, case study, survey, site review, etc.?

____ Instrumentation

What information gathering instruments and techniques will be used?

____ Sampling

What samples will be drawn, and how will they be drawn?

____ Information gathering

How will the information gathering plan be implemented, and who will gather the information?

____ Data storage and retrieval

What format, procedures, and facilities will be used to store and retrieve the information?

____ Data analysis

How will the information be analyzed?

____ Reporting

What reports and techniques will be used to disseminate the findings?

____ Technical adequacy

To what degree will the needs assessment information be reliable, valid, and objective?

*Management Plan*

____ Organizational mechanism

What organizational unit will be used to do the needs assessment (an in-house office of evaluation, a self evaluation system, a contract with an external agency, a consortium-supported evaluation center, etc.)?

____ Organizational location

Through what channels could the needs assessment influence policy formulation and administrative decision making?

____ Policies and procedures

What established and/or ad hoc policies and procedures will govern this needs assessment?

____ Staff

How will the needs assessment be staffed?

____ Facilities

What space, equipment, and materials will be available to support the needs assessment?

____ Data-gathering schedule

What instruments will be administered, to what groups, according to what schedule?

____ Reporting schedule

What reports will be provided,

to what audiences, according to what schedule?

____ Training

What training will be provided to what groups and who will provide it?

____ Installation of needs assessment

Will this needs assessment be used to aid the system to improve and extend its internal capability to assess needs?

____ Budget

What is the internal structure of the budget? How will it be monitored?

*Moral/Ethical/Utility Questions*

____ Philosophical stance

What is the values base for the needs assessment?

____ Service orientation

What social good, if any, will be served by this needs assessment and whose values will be served?

____ Asessor's values

Will the needs assessor's technical standards and his values conflict with the client's systems and/or sponsor's values? Will the needs assessor face any conflict of interest problems? What will be done about possible conflicts?

____ Judgments

Will the needs assessor identify needs or leave that up to the client? Or will the assessor obtain, analyze, and report the judgments of various reference groups?

____ Objectivity

How will the needs assessor avoid being coopted and maintain his objectivity?

____ Prospects for utility

Will the needs assessment meet utility criteria (see evaluation standards)?

____ Cost/effectiveness

Compared to its potential payoff, will the needs assessment be implemented at a reasonable cost?

# APPENDIX 6B
# CHECKLIST FOR JUDGING
# THE ADEQUACY OF
# AN EVALUATION DESIGN
## By: James Sanders and Dean Nafziger

*Directions*: For each question below, circle whether the evaluation design has clearly met the criterion (Yes), has clearly not met the criterion (No), or cannot be clearly determined (?). Circle *NA* if the criterion does not apply to the evaluation design being reviewed. Use the *Elaboration* column to provide further explanation when a *No* or a *?* has been circled.

Description of Evaluation Study: _____

Name of Reviewer: _____

| *Criterion* | *Criterion Met* | *Elaboration* |
|---|---|---|

I. Regarding the Adequacy of the
   Evaluation Conceptualization

   A. *Scope*: Does the range of information
      to be provided include all the signifi-
      cant aspects of the program or
      product being evaluated?
      1. Is a description of the program or
         product presented (e.g.,

philosophy, content, objec-
tives, procedures, setting)? Yes No ? NA

2. Are the intended outcomes
of the program or product
specified and does the evaluation
address them? Yes No ? NA

3. Are any likely unintended effects
from the program or product
considered? Yes No ? NA

4. Is cost information about the
program or product included? Yes No ? NA

B. *Relevance*: Does the information to
be provided adequately serve the
evaluation needs of the intended
audiences?

1. Are the audiences for the
evaluation identified? Yes No ? NA

2. Are the objectives of the
evaluation explained? Yes No ? NA

3. Are the objectives of the
evaluation congruent with the
information needs of the intended
audiences? Yes No ? NA

4. Does the information to be
provided allow necessary
decisions about the program or
product to be made? Yes No ? NA

C. *Flexibility*: Does the evaluation
study allow for new information
needs to be met as they arise?

1. Can the design be adapted easily
to accommodate new needs? Yes No ? NA

2. Are known constraints on the
evaluation discussed? Yes No ? NA

3. Can useful information be
obtained in the face of unforeseen
constraints, e.g., noncooperation
of control groups? Yes No ? NA

D. *Feasibility*: Can the evaluation be
carried out as planned?

1. Are the evaluation resources
(time, money, and personnel)
adequate to carry out the

projected activities?      Yes  No  ?  NA

2. Are management plans specified for conducting evaluation?      Yes  No  ?  NA

3. Has adequate planning been done to support the feasibility of particularly difficult activities?      Yes  No  ?  NA

---

II. Criteria Concerning the Adequacy of the Collection and Processing of Information

A. *Reliability*: Is the information to be collected in a manner such that findings are replicable?

1. Are data collection procedures described well enough to be followed by others?      Yes  No  ?  NA

2. Are scoring or coding procedures objective?      Yes  No  ?  NA

3. Are the evaluation instruments reliable?      Yes  No  ?  NA

B. *Objectivity*: Have attempts been made to control for bias in data collection and processing?

1. Are sources of information clearly specified?      Yes  No  ?  NA

2. Are possible biases on the part of data collectors adequately controlled?      Yes  No  ?  NA

C. *Representativeness*: Do the information collection and processing procedures ensure that the results accurately portray the program or product?

1. Are the data collection instruments valid?      Yes  No  ?  NA

2. Are the data collection instruments appropriate for the purposes of this evaluation?      Yes  No  ?  NA

3. Does the evaluation design adequately address the questions it was intended to answer?      Yes  No  ?  NA

III. Criteria Concerning the Adequacy of
the Presentation and Reporting of
Information

A. *Timeliness*: Is the information
provided timely enough to be of use
to the audiences for the evaluation?
1. Does the time schedule for
reporting meet the needs of the
audiences?                                    Yes   No   ?   NA
2. Is the reporting schedule shown to
be appropriate for the schedule of
decisions?                                    Yes   No   ?   NA

B. *Pervasiveness*: Is information to be
provided to all who need it?
1. Is information to be disseminated   Yes   No   ?   NA
to all intended audiences?
2. Are attempts being made to make
the evaluation information
available to relevant audiences
beyond those directly affected by
the evaluation?                               Yes   No   ?   NA

IV. General Criteria

A. *Ethical Considerations*: Does the
intended evaluation study strictly
follow accepted ethical standards?
1. Do test administration procedures
follow professional standards of
ethics?                                       Yes   No   ?   NA
2. Have protection of human
subjects guidelines been
followed?                                     Yes   No   ?   NA
3. Has confidentiality of data been
guaranteed?                                   Yes   No   ?   NA

B. *Protocol*: Are appropriate protocol
steps planned?
1. Are appropriate persons
contacted in the appropriate
sequence?                                     Yes   No   ?   NA
2. Are department policies and
procedures to be followed?                    Yes   No   ?   NA

# APPENDIX A
# ESTABLISHING VALIDITY
# AND RELIABILITY
# IN INSTRUMENTATION

Validity and reliability are characteristics that must be present in your efforts to collect and intepret data or you risk collecting information too inaccurate to be usable.

*Validity* refers to how truthful, genuine, and authentic data are in representing what they purport to measure. To be valid is to make truthful claims. To be valid, instruments must measure what the investigator intends and claims to measure. Data produced by instruments must authentically represent the traits and phenomena you use them to represent.

*Reliability* is related to the accuracy of measures. The more error in a measure, the more unreliable it is. Reliability means different things in different kinds of measures, but in general it represents the trustworthiness of data produced. We might know that a bathroom scale, for instance, is capable of producing indications of weight: the number of points is a measure of weight. But if the bathroom scale's indicator slips and is loose and its viewing glass is scratched and dirty, it is highly likely that it will give anyone weighing himself repeatedly different and erroneous results. The scale is unreliable.

Reliability and validity are achieved through the careful design, testing, and revision of instruments and information collection procedures.

## Kinds of Validity and Reliability

### Types of Validity

There are four general applications of the term *validity* that are used among educators: content validity, concurrent validity, predictive validity, and construct validity. More recently, with the advent of minimum competency testing and court challenges to validity, the notion of "curricular" validity has gained currency. (See George F. Madaus, *The Courts, Validity and Minimum Competency Testing* [Boston: Kluwer-Nijhoff Publishing, 1983] for a current discussion of validity.) But all types of validity spring from the same basic concept: information should authentically represent what it purports to and what it is used for.

**Content validity.** Does an instrument contain the appropriate content? Are test items consistent with school curriculum? Are the behaviors listed in a teacher observation related to teaching ability? Do rating items for a program design evaluation represent a meaningful range of criteria?

**Concurrent validity.** Does a measure produce results consistent with some other independent measure? (For example, do self-ratings of knowledge correlate with scores on a knowledge test?)

**Predictive validity.** This is the ability of a measure to faithfully predict some other future trait or measure. (For example, does a score on the interview for a teaching position predict success as a teacher?)

**Construct validity.** This refers to data whether from the use of the instrument faithfully represents the intended theoretical construct and requires considerable research to establish and investigate. An example of construct validity inquiry would be research to determine if persons who achieve poor scores on a test of workshop objectives are in fact, different in producing the intended behaviors in their work.

**Curricular validity.** Most measurement practitioners have construed content validity to be the fit between a test and a curriculum's objectives. This definition, however, did not include consideration of whether what was on a test had in fact been taught to pupils. Thus, a variant of content validity has become thought of as curricular validity. Curricular validity relates to the extent to which a test measures what was actually taught to pupils and thus includes consideration of the *fairness* of a test.

*Types of Reliability*

**Stability or repeatability.**  A test or measure that provides consistent scores from instance to instance is reliable, that is, stable over time. A content rating of an IEP, for instance, should not produce different scores for the same IEP depending on when and where the analysis takes place.

**Interjudge or interrater agreement.**  A rating should reflect the characteristics of the object being rated, not the vagaries and differences among users of the instrument (the judges). This kind of reliability is vastly improved by training raters and judges.

**Equivalency.**  This refers to the degree of consistency between two alternate forms of the "same" test or measure. If tests are equivalent (produce the same scores), then differences over time (e.g., after a class) can be inferred to be the result of instruction, not the result of having taken the test before.

**Internal consistency.**  This refers to how well a group of items on a measure "hang together." It tells how unidimensional the measure is— whether items are measuring one trait. Estimates of this kind of reliability can be made by checking the degree of correlation between split-halves of the test, or other measures requiring only one administration of the test.

## Procedures for Increasing Reliability and Validity

In thinking about how to increase the reliability and validity of your data collection efforts, you should recognize and keep two facts up front.

- Neither reliability nor validity is a one-time phenomenon. You must be continually aware of them, working to increase them and deal with problems that arise throughout the life of a needs assessment.

- There is no a priori level of minimum reliability or validity that can be set for your measures. The more you increase these characteristics, the more sure you can be of your results, and you can use them with more confidence.

*Some General Steps and Considerations*

**Validity and how you use data.**  Validity is not so much a characteristic intrinsic to some data, but is more related to how you *use* data. Self-ratings of knowledge are known, for example, to be quite an accurate estimation of actual knowledge. To use self-ratings in a certification program as a basis for grading, however, would likely be an invalid use. Use of self-ratings in an inservice workshop, however, as a means for participants to select paths of study, would be far more valid.

Consider, then, how you will use the information. Will it provide a genuine and authentic measure of what you want *to use it for*? Could it easily be contaminated by another factor (as in the case of self-rating for certification)?

**Achieving content validity.**  When constructing a test, rating scale, questionnaire, checklist, or behavioral observation, you need to be sure that the items on the form are measuring the appropriate content. This is largely a judgment issue. Seek advice from colleagues, experts, literature, and research; observe the curriculum-in-practice. Ask:

- Does the content reflect what is important in this school, course, program, etc.?

- Is there agreement that these variables are important?

- Does the literature, other programs, or research support these variables as being correct?

- Is there a logical connection between what you are measuring and what you need to know?

- Is there evidence that what is to be measured is indeed being taught?

**Maintaining validity.**  Because validity is related to how data get *used*, you need to monitor and reflect on the uses of data you collect to avoid invalid applications. A principal should not, for example, use grades assigned to pupils to compare teachers as to whose students are learning the most. Nor should an inservice coordinator base decisions of who in the district needs what training on preferences expressed from a volunteer survey.

An intended use could be quite valid; an actual use could be quite invalid. Monitoring usage of data, facilitating interpretation (See the "Reporting" chapter), and exploring meaning in data empirically and reflectively will increase validity, and the utility of your evaluation.

**Designing instruments for reliability.**  Reliability is related to error in measuring. An instrument that is unclear, vague, confusing, and difficult to use, is bound to be unreliable. You can achieve needed levels of reliability very often by trying out an instrument, and revising it based on feedback.

- Make sure directions are clear.
- Be sure there is only one way to respond to and interpret an item.
- Eliminate items with dual stems (like "How useful and interesting was the workshop?")

**Monitor data collection to insure quality control.** Instruments used differently in different situations will produce nonparallel, unreliable data. You need to be sure that data collection gets carried out the way it was intended and that it is consistent from instance to instance.

**Train experts, judges, and raters when you use rating instruments; know your judges.** Without training and adequate direction, raters are likely to apply varying criteria and to see different things. If you want to treat their data equivalently, then you must train them. If you plan to use their judgments independently, you need to know what rules they used, the criteria they applied, their perspectives, etc. so you can interpret their opinions reliably.

**To enhance the reliability of ratings, use increasingly specific rating variables.** Global judgments (for example, "How effective is this teacher?") can easily be unreliable. To get more precision into your data, break the global concept into several subconcepts.

# APPENDIX B
# TECHNIQUES FOR ANALYZING
# NEEDS ASSESSMENT
# INFORMATION

## Descriptive Statistics

The technique perhaps most frequently used in analyzing data pertaining to primary needs is descriptive statistics. This technique involves looking at typical performance through the use of means, medians, and modes; the variability of performance through computation of frequency distributions, variances, standard deviations, and the identification of the range of scores. Descriptive statistics usually is applied to performance at a given time by groups and subgroups, but may be applied to multiple performances over time by an individual.

The application of the technique usually involves the following steps. The assessors must first identify the set of scores to be described, such as the scores of a group of fifth grade students on a given achievement test. They might arrange the scores in a frequency distribution and could add them and divide them by the number of scores to obtain the average or mean performance of the group. They could also identify the median of the distribution (the point above and below which half the scores fall) and the mode (the score with the highest frequency of occurrence). They could identify the range of scores (the difference between the lowest and the highest scores). And, they could compute the standard deviation of the

211

scores (the square root of the sum of squared deviations of all scores from the mean of the distribution) to obtain an indication of the spread of scores in the distribution.

Descriptive statistics are very useful in a wide range of needs assessment studies. In general, they provide an efficient means of summarizing large quantities of data that would otherwise be uninterpretable and also provide the basis for more sophisticated analyses. Explanations of these descriptive statistics are available in standard introductory statistics texts.

## Suggested Readings

Ary, D., and Jacobs, L.C. *Introduction to Statistics: A Systems Approach.* New York: Holt, Rinehart and Winston, 1976.
Downie, N.M., and Starry, A.R. *Descriptive and Inferential Statistics.* New York: Harper & Row, 1977.

## Inferential Statistics

As the name implies, inferential statistical methods assist you in drawing conclusions or making inferences about a given population from data on a sample of that population. A wide range of statistical procedures are included in this category: analysis of variance (ANOVA), discriminant analysis, linear regression analysis, correlation, path analysis, multivariate analysis of variance (MANOVA), factor analysis, and others. These techniques help you address questions such as:

1. Is there a relationship between socioeconomic background and reading achievement?
2. Do students in program X perform better than students in program Y?
3. Do students in the affective development program change their attitude toward school from the beginning of the year to the end of the year?
4. Are the program entrance criteria effective in selecting students who will be successful in the program?
5. Do students perform differently on a test of motor skill and speed at different time periods during the day?

Computer software packages are available to calculate a wide range of descriptive and inferential statistics. One of the most widely used collections of such programs is the Statistical Package for the Social Sciences (SPSS).

The SPSS manual will describe the various programs and how to use them.

Although computer programs will handle all the necessary calculations for complex procedures, selection of the appropriate inferential statistical method and accurate interpretation of the results demand a high level of statistical expertise. Novices should consult a knowledgeable and experienced data analyst.

## Suggested Readings

Edwards, A.L. *An Introduction to Linear Regression and Correlation*. San Francisco: Freeman, 1976.

Fink, A., and Kosecoff, J. (Eds.). *How To Evaluate Educational Programs: A Monthly Guide to Methods and Ideas that Work* (Vol. 3, no. 2) Washington, D.C.: Capital Publications, 1980. For information contact: Emily C. Harris, Editorial Director, Capital Publications, Inc., 2430 Pennsylvania Ave., N.W., Washington, D.C. 20037, 202-452-1600. (Monthly publications from previous years are available in bound form.)

Guilford, J.P., and Fruchter, B. *Fundamental Statistics in Psychology and Education*. New York: McGraw-Hill, 1978.

Kerlinger, F.N., and Pedhazur, E.J. *Multiple Regression in Behavioral Research*. New York: Holt, Rinehart and Winston, 1973.

## Adversary/Advocacy Teams

This technique is analogous to a public debate or jury trial. Members are assigned to either the adversary or advocacy team. A jury or panel of judges is selected to review the position papers and oral presentations presented by each team and to provide a recommended action statement. In education the panel may consist of the school board, a planning committee, selected experts in a given field, district personnel who will be charged with implementing a selected program or procedure. The teams and panel meet initially to define the issues and establish the ground rules for the procedure. Each team then collects and organizes pertinent data and develops arguments and theories to explain their position. A written brief stating the team's position and factual support for that position is prepared. Each team makes an oral presentation to the panel of judges summarizing the written brief. During the presentations, judges have the opportunity to ask questions. Based on the written and oral presentation, judges then render an opinion or recommend a course of action.

## Suggested Readings

Owens, T. Educational Evaluation by Adversary Proceeding. In E. House (Ed.), *School Evaluation: The Politics and Process.* Berkeley, CA: McCutchan, 1973.

Popham, W.J., and Carlson, D. Deep dark deficits of the adversary evaluation models. *Educational Researcher* 6(6):3–6, 1977.

Thurston, P. Revitalizing adversary evaluations: Deep dark deficits or muddled mistaken musings. *Educational Researcher* 7(7):3–8, 1978.

Wolf, R.L., and Arnstein, G. Trial by jury: A new evaluation method. *Phi Delta Kappan* 57(3):185–190, 1975.

## Content Analysis

Content analysis is a general analysis technique for use in reducing complex narrative information (transcriptions of meetings, court rulings, position papers, newspaper accounts, and so forth) to simpler terms (a list of issues, key assumptions, proposed outcomes, alleged problems). The outcome of a content analysis might be simply the list of items that were identified, a frequency distribution of the numbers of times each item was mentioned, a taxonomy based on the items, a matrix that relates the items to one or more other variables, or an index that indicates how much of some characteristic is present in the information.

The process of content analysis is general and adaptable depending on the question to be answered. The process may be open and exploratory, as when the assessor is searching for the main educational issues that are reflected in a set of newspaper editorials without any predilections about what the issues might be. Sometimes the process is closed and structured, as in the classification of objectives in teachers' lesson plans in relation to a given taxonomy of educational objectives. Often the process combines open and closed analysis by first searching out issues (an open-ended activity) and then organizing and assessing them against some selected logical structure (a closed and structured activity.)

Consider an analysis of individual educational plans of third grade students to identify and examine the referenced learning problems:

1.  What range of learning problems are mentioned? As the plans are read, each problem mentioned might be listed on a separate index card along with the identification number of the plan in which it appeared. Like problems with similar wording could then be combined, and the problems could be listed for presentation.

2.  What types of problems were identified? The cards might be studied to develop an outline of the types and subtypes of problems that were identified, for example, motivation, attention span, reading for main idea, study habits. Or the cards might be sorted into predetermined categories of problems, such as intellectual, aesthetic, social, vocational, emotional, physical, and moral.
3.  Which problem areas are addressed most frequently? The number of plans citing problems in each area could be determined, and the numbers could be converted to proportions of the total number of cited problems.

The preceding is but one example of how content analysis might be employed in educational needs assessments. Other examples include investigating the contents of achievement tests, job descriptions, state plans, and minutes of meetings of parent-teacher associations. Content analysis of such items of information might be done to address a variety of questions that are important in needs assessments: What educational objectives are implicit in the material? Which of the objectives seem to be receiving priority attention? What are the main complaints about existing services?

Overall, content analysis is a general, adaptable technique that may be used to study complex information items in order to extract, organize, and summarize meanings in specified areas. The key steps are to identify the sources of information to be explored, to focus the analysis on specified questions, and to devise and execute a systematic strategy for extracting, organizing, and summarizing answers to the questions.

Additional information about content analysis may be obtained from the following references.

## Suggested Readings

Berelson, B. Content Analysis. In G. Lindzey (Ed.), *Handbook of Social Psychology* (vol. 1). Reading, MA: Addison-Wesley, 1954, pp. 488–522.

Guilford, J., and Fruchter, B. *Fundamental Statistics in Psychology and Education.* New York: McGraw-Hill, 1978.

Hopkins, K., and Glass, *Basic Statistics for the Behavioral Sciences* . Englewood Cliffs, NJ: Prentice-Hall, 1978.

Kerlinger, F. *Foundations of Behavioral Research*. New York: Holt, Rinehart and Winston, 1965.

**Delphi Technique**

The Delphi technique is designed to obtain group consensus among people with a wide range of diverse opinions. This technique is appropriate when seeking answers to questions such as:

1.  What are primary goals of the school district?
2.  What questions should be addressed in the needs assessment?
3.  What basic competencies should students master prior to graduation?

The technique entails collecting opinions from the target audiences on items to be considered. One then makes a master list of items and asks the group to rate or rank items in order of importance. The process of tabulating responses and then prioritizing items is repeated until consensus is reached. All responses are kept anonymous. Data are reported by group. No individual opinions are identified.

*Example*

A district is in the process of developing a five-year plan. The first step is to develop a district philosophy and set of major goals. A needs assessment will then be conducted to determine how well the district is achieving the stated goals and what needs should be addressed during the next five years.

A group of 20 representatives of the business community, teaching staff, parents, students, and administration are selected to develop a list of goals to be included in a survey instrument. Each member is asked to list the goals he or she considers to be primary goals for the district. The lists are collected and the 40 most frequently listed goals are selected.

The items are listed on a questionnaire with these instructions provided:

> The following list of goals was compiled by the district planning committee. Please review each item and rank the 10 goals you feel are most important, 1 = most important, 2 = second most, etc.

After the surveys were completed, the rankings were assigned points (1 = 10 points, 2 = 9 points ... 10 = 1 point). The points were tallied for each item and the results returned to the respondents for their review. They were asked to either join the emerging consensus, as revealed by the top ten rated items, or to indicate in writing why the other respondents should change their ratings. The second set of ratings plus the written reactions were then distributed to all respondents with the request to review their ratings and submit either a confirmation of what they had previously done or a set of revised ratings.

## Suggested Readings

Dalkey, N.C. *The Delphi Method: An Experimental Study of Group Opinion.* Santa Monica, CA: Rand Corporation, 1969.
Fink, A., and Kosecoff, J. (Eds.). *How To Evaluate Educational Programs*, Chapter 46. Washington, D.C.: Capital Publications, 1981.
Linstone, H.A., and Turoff, M. *The Delphi Method: Techniques and Applications.* Reading, MA: Addison-Wesley, 1975.

## Goal Attainment Scaling

Goal attainment scaling is a form of evaluation commonly used in social service areas. It was developed by Thomas Kiresuk and Robert Sherman at the Hennepin Mental Health Center in Minneapolis, Minnesota. This method of evaluation consists of four basic steps:

1. List goals.
2. Develop a scale that lists specific outcome behaviors at each point.
3. Weight each goal according to its importance.
4. After completion of the program or a designated time period, rate achievement on each goal and calculate a single goal attainment score for all goals.

A sample goal attainment scale is provided in Table B-1. Expected level of achievement is always given a value of zero. Scale headings identify the aspect of functioning the scale is intended to measure. Scale weights are numbers assigned to each goal to reflect the relative importance of each goal. Weight numbers may be any number from 1–100, and the total of the weights do not have to equal 100. For each scale, you must define a total of 2 to 5 points. Each point description must be specific and so well defined that an impartial person will be able to accurately and reliably determine the subject's level of achievement on each goal. After six months in an intensive rehabilitation program, the individual was rated on achievement of each goal by an evaluator not associated with the program: Score for

Table B-1. Sample Goal Attainment Scale

| Scale Attainment Level | Scale 1: Mobility (weight = 20) | Scale 2: Expressive Communication (weight = 30) |
|---|---|---|
| Most unfavorable: X = −2 | Wheelchair-bound full time—no assistance required | Total reliance on communication board for expressive communication |
| Less than expected: X = −1 | Ambulation with walker and full leg braces—assistance required full time for stability | Communicates needs with combination of one syllable words and gestures |
| Expected: X = 0 | Ambulation with walker and full leg braces—no assistance required | Communicates needs verbally in one word intelligible utterances |
| More than expected: X = 1 | Ambulation with full leg braces—assistance required full-time for stability | Communicates verbally in two word intelligible phrases |
| Most favorable: X = 2 | Ambulation with full leg braces—no assistance required | Communicates in three word intelligible phrases |

goal 1 = 0; score for goal 2 = +2. The goal attainment score was then calculated using the following formula:

$$\text{Goal attainment score} = 50 + \frac{10\sum w_i x_i}{.7\sum w_i^2 + .3\left(\sum w_i\right)^2}$$

(w = weight; x = goal score)

$$\text{G.A.S.} = 50 + \frac{10(w_1 x_1 + w_2 x_2)}{\sqrt{.7[w_1^2 + w_2^2] + .3(w_1 + w_2)^2}}$$

$$= 50 + \frac{10[20(0) + 30(2)]}{\sqrt{.7[(20)^2 + (30)^2] + .3(20 + 30)^2}}$$

$$= 50 + \frac{10[0 + 60]}{\sqrt{.7(400 + 900) + .3(50)^2}}$$

$$= 50 + \frac{600}{\sqrt{.7(1300) + .3(2500)}}$$

$$= 50 + \frac{600}{\sqrt{910 + 750}}$$

$$= 50 + \frac{600}{\sqrt{1660}}$$

$$= 50 + \frac{600}{\sqrt{40.743097}}$$

$$= 50 + 14.73$$

$$= 64.73$$

The goal attainment score can be utilized to compare treatment outcomes for a wide variety of handicapping conditions, types of individuals, etc., and widely differing treatment modes, such as a self-contained classroom, itinerant services, an outpatient clinic, a specific remedial program, etc. The process provides information that is useful to the teacher or therapist and also to the administrator in evaluating agency services and programs.

## Suggested Readings

Kiresuk, T.J., and Lund, S.H. Process and Outcome Measurement Using Goal Attainment Scaling. In J. Zusman and C.R. Weirster (Eds.), *Program Evaluation: Alcohol, Drug Abuse and Mental Health Services*. Lexington, MA: Lexington Books, 1975.

Kiresuk, T.J., and Sherman, R.E. Goal attainment scaling: A general method for evaluating comprehensive mental health programs. *Community Mental Health Journal* 4(6):443–453, 1968.

Program Evaluation Resource Center
501 Park Avenue South
Minneapolis, MN 55415

# BIBLIOGRAPHY

Alkin, M.C., Daillak, R., and White, P. *Using Evaluations: Does Evaluation Make a Difference?* Beverly Hills: Sage, 1979.

Anderson, S.C. et al. *Encyclopedia of Educational Evaluation.* San Francisco: Jossey-Bass, 1975.

Ary, D., and Jacobs, L.C. Introduction to Statistics: A Systems Approach. New York: Holt, Rinehart and Winston, 1976.

Babbie, E.R. *Survey Research Methods.* Belmont, CA: Wadsworth, 1973.

Berelson, B. Content Analysis. In G. Lindzey (Ed.), *Handbook of Social Psychology* (vol. 1). Reading, MA: Addison Wesley, 1954, pp. 488–522.

Bickel, W.E., and Coaley, W.W. *The Utilization of a District-Wide Needs Assessment.* Research Report, Learning Research and Development Center, University of Pittsburgh, 1981.

Bode, B.H. *Democracy as a Way of Life.* New York: Macmillan, 1937.

Bode, B.H. *Progressive Education at the Crossroads.* New York: Newson & Company, 1933, pp 62–72.

Braskamp, L.A., Brown, R.D., and Newman, D.L. *Studying Evaluation Utilization Through Simulations.* Unpublished paper, University of Illinois at Urbana, Champaign, and University of Nebraska-Lincoln, undated.

Bruyn, S.T. *The Human Perspective in Sociology: The Methodology of Participation Observation.* Englewood Cliffs, NJ: Prentice-Hall, 1966.

Clayton, A.S. *Historical and Social Determinants of Public Education Policy in the United States and Europe.* Bloomington, IN: Indiana University, 1965.

221

Coffing, R.T., and Hutchison, T.E. *Needs Analysis Methodology: A Prescriptive Set of Rules and Procedures for Identifying, Defining, and Measuring Needs.* Paper presented to the American Educational Research Association San Francisco, April 17, 1979.

Dalkey, N.C. *The Delphi Method: An Experimental Study of Group Opinion.* Santa Monica, CA: Rand Corporation, 1969.

Davis, B. (Ed.). *Evaluation News #8: Proceedings Issue—Fourth Annual Conference.* San Francisco: Evaluation Institute, University of San Francisco, December 1978.

Demaline, R.E., and Quinn, D.W. *Hints for Planning and Conducting a Survey and Bibliography of Survey Methods.* Kalamazoo, MI: Evaluation Center, Western Michigan University, 1979.

Downie, N.M., and Starry, A.R. *Descriptive and Inferential Statistics.* New York: Harper & Row, 1977.

Ebel, R.L. *Measuring Educational Achievement.* Englewood Cliffs, NJ: Prentice-Hall, 1965.

*Educational Technology* 17(11): November, 1977. This is a special issue that contains a series of articles on various aspects of the concept and practice of needs assessment.

Edwards, A.L. *An Introduction to Linear Regression and Correlation.* San Francisco: Freeman, 1976.

English, F.W. The politics of needs assessment. *Educational Technology* 17(11): November, 1977.

Fink, A., and Kosecoff, J. (Eds.). *How to Evaluate Education Programs: A Monthly Guide to Methods and Ideas That Work* (vol. 3, no. 2). Washington, D.C.: Capitol Publications, February, 1980.

Flesch, R. *On Business Communication: How to Say What You Mean in Plain English.* New York: Harper & Row, 1972.

Furst, N.J. Systematic Classroom Observation. In L. Deighten (Ed.), *Encyclopedia of Education.* New York: Macmillan, 1971.

Gove, P.B., et al. (Eds.). *Webster's Third International Dictionary.* Springfield, MA: G. & C. Merriam Co., 1976.

Gronlund, N.E. *Constructing Achievement Tests.* Englewood Cliffs, NJ: Prentice-Hall, 1968.

Guba, E.G., and Lincoln, Y.S. *Effective Evaluation: Improving the Usefulness of Evaluation Results Through Responsive and Naturalistic Approaches.* San Francisco: Jossey-Bass, 1981.

Guba, E.G., and Lincoln, Y.S. The place of values in needs assessment. *Educational Evaluation and Policy Analysis* 5(2): Winter, 1982.

Guilford, J.P., and Fruchter, B. *Fundamental Statistics in Psychology and Education.* New York: McGraw-Hill, 1978.

Hargan, M., and Farringer, P. *Special Education: A Guide to Needs Assessment.* Westport, CN: Market Data Retrieval, 1977.

Hargreaves, W.A., Attkisson, C.C., and Sorenson, J.E. (Eds.). Reviews of Needs

Assessment and Planning Monographs. In *Resource Materials for Community Mental Health Program Evaluation* (2nd ed.), 1977.

Hawkridge, D.G., Campeau, P.L., and Trickett, P.K. *Preparing Evaluation Reports: A Guide for Authors.* AIR Monograph no. 6. Pittsburgh: American Institutes for Research, 1970.

Hopkins, K., and Glass, G. *Basic Statistics for the Behavioral Sciences.* Englewood Cliffs, NJ: Prentice -Hall, 1978.

Huba, M.E., McNally, E.F., and Netusil, A.J. *Perceived Effectiveness of the PDK Needs Assessment Model in Selected Iowa School Districts.* Paper presented to the American Educational Research Association, San Francisco, April 1979.

Illinois Office of Education. Evaluation and Assessment Section. Needs Assessment Process Outline. Springfield, IL.

Iowa Valley Community College District. *Career Education Needs Assessment for Merged Area VI.* Marshalltown, IA: Iowa Valley Community College District, 1975.

Joint Committee on Standards for Educational Evaluation *Standards for Evaluations of Educational Programs, Projects, and Materials.* New York: McGraw-Hill, 1981.

Kaufman, R., and English, F.W. *Needs Assessment: Concept and Application.* Englewood Cliffs, NJ: Educational Technology Publishers, 1979.

Kaufman, R.A. *Educational System Planning.* Englewood Cliffs, NJ: Prentice-Hall, 1972.

Kearney, C.P., and Harper, R.J. The Politics of Reporting Results. In E.R. House (Ed.), *School Evaluation: The Politics and Process.* Berkeley, CA: McCutchan, 1973.

Kerlinger, F. *Foundations of Behavioral Research.* New York: Holt, Rinehart and Winston, 1965.

Kerlinger, F.N., and Pedhazur, E.J. *Multiple Regression in Behavioral Research.* New York: Holt, Rinehart and Winston, 1973.

Kimmel, W. *A Needs Assessment: A Critical Perspective.* Washington, D.C.: Office of Program Systems, Office of the Assistant Secretary for Planning and Evaluation, Department of Health, Education, and Welfare, 1977.

Kiresuk, T.J., and Lund, S.H. Process and Outcome Measurement Using Goal Attainment Scaling. In J. Zusman and C.R. Weirster (Eds.), *Program Evaluation: Alcohol, Drug Abuse and Mental Health Services.* Lexington, MA: Lexington Books, 1975.

Kiresuk, T.J., and Sherman, R.E. Goal attainment scaling: A general method for evaluating comprehensive mental health programs. *Community Mental Health Journal* 4(6): 1968.

Kominski, E.S. *Educational Needs Assessments: Discrepancies Between Theory and Practice.* Paper presented to the American Educational Research Association, San Francisco, April 1979.

Lamberti, J., and Pratt, R. *Instructional Assessment.* Arlington, VA: ERIC Document Reproduction Service, ED 152 708, 1978.

Lanham, R.A. *Revising Prose*. New York: Scribners, 1978.

Leonard, E.C., Jr. *Assessment of Training Needs*. Fort Wayne, In: City of Fort Wayne, Midwest Intergovernmental Training Committee, 1974.

Linstone, H.A., and Turoff, M. *The Delphi Method: Techniques and Applications*. Reading, MA: Addison-Wesley, 1975.

Madaus, G.F. *The Courts, Validity and Minimum Competency Testing*. Boston, MA: Kluwer-Nijhoff Publishing, 1983.

McCall, K.M. *Educational Needs Assessment*. Upper Darby, PA: Upper Darby School District, SPEEDIER Project, 1977.

Morris, L.L., and Fitz-Gibbon, C.T. *Evaluators Handbook*. Beverly Hills, CA: Sage, 1978.

Myers, E.C., & Koenigs, S.S. *A Framework for Comparing Needs Assessment Activities*. Paper presented to the American Educational Research Association, San Francisco, April 1979.

National Association of State Directors of Special Education. *The Prince William Model: A Planning Guide for the Development and Implementation of Full Services for All Handicapped Children*. Washington, D.C.: National Association of State Directors of Special Education, 1976.

Nguyen, T.D., and Attkisson, C.C. *Theoretical Issues in Defining and Identifying Human Service Needs*. Paper presented to the American Psychological Association, San Francisco, August 26–September 1, 1977.

Office of Program Evaluation and Research. *Handbook for Reporting and Using Test Results*. Sacramento: California State Department of Education, 1979.

Olson, T.A. *Needs Assessment from the Perspective of a Regional Educational Laboratory*. Paper presented to the American Educational Research Association, San Francisco, April 1979.

Owens, T. Educational Evaluation by Adversary Proceeding. In E. House (Ed.), *School Evaluation: The Politics and Process*. Berkeley, CA: McCutchan, 1973. 1973.

Patterson, J.L., and Czajkowski, T.J. District needs assessment: One avenue to program improvement. *Phi Delta Kappan*, December, 1976. 327–329.

Patton, M.Q. *Utilization-Focused Evaluation*. Beverly Hills, CA: Sage, 1978.

Patton, M.Q. *Qualitative Evaluation Methods*. Beverly Hills, CA: Sage, 1980.

Payne, S.L. *The Art of Asking Questions*. Princeton, NJ: Princeton University Press, 1951.

Pennsylvania State Department of Education. *Suggested Methods for the Identification of Critical Goals*. Harrisburg, PA: 1975.

Popham, W.J. *Educational Evaluation*. Englewood Cliffs, NJ: Prentice-Hall, 1975.

Popham, W.J., and Carlson, D. Deep dark deficits of the adversary evaluation model. *Educational Researcher*, 6(6): 3–6, 1977.

Price, N.C. et al. (Eds.). *Comprehensive Needs Assessment*. Redwood City, CA: San Mateo County Office of Education, Educational Support and Planning Division, 1977.

Program Development Center of Northern California. *Educational Planning Model: Individual Rating of the Level of Performance of Current School Programs*. Bloomington, IN: Phi Delta Kappa, 1976.

Program Development Center of Northern California. *Educational Planning Model: Phase I Forms*. Bloomington, IN: Phi Delta Kappa.

Program Development Center of Northern California. *Educational Planning Model: Phase I Manual*. Bloomington, IN: Phi Delta Kappa.

Program Development Center of Northern California. *Educational Planning Model, Phase II: Curriculum Development Manual, Revised*. Bloomington, IN: Phi Delta Kappa, 1978.

Program Development Center of Northern California. *Educational Planning Model, Phase II: Programmed Course for Writing Performance Objectives, Revised*. Bloomington, IN: Phi Delta Kappa, 1978.

Program Development Center of Northern California. *Educational Planning Model, Phase III: A Program for Community and Professional Involvement*. Bloomington, IN: Phi Delta Kappa.

Program Development Center of Northern California. *Educational Planning Model, Phase III Forms*. Bloomington, IN: Phi Delta Kappan.

Randall, J.H. Jr., and Buchler, A. *Philosophy: An Introduction*. New York: Barnes and Noble, 1960.

Richardson, S., Dohrenwend, H.S., and Klein, D. *Interviewing: Its Forms and Functions*. New York: Basic Books, 1965.

Rookey, T.J. *Needs Assessment Model: East Stroudsburg-Project NAMES Workbook*. Arlington, VA: ERIC Document Reproduction Service, ED 133 828, 1976.

Rose, C., and Nyre, C.F. *The Practice of Evaluation: ERIC/TM Report 65*. Princeton, NJ: ERIC Clearinghouse on Tests, Measurement, and Evaluation, Educational Testing Service, December, 1977.

Rossi, P.H., Freeman, H.E., and Wright, S.R. *Evaluation: A Systematic Approach*. Beverly Hills, CA: Sage, 1979.

Roth, J.E. Needs and the needs assessment process. *Evaluation News #5*. December 1977, 15–17.

Roth, J.E. *Needs Assessment Bibliography*. San Francisco: University of San Francisco, Evaluation Institute.

Roth, J.E. *Theory and Practice of Needs Assessment with Special Application to Institutes of Higher Learning*. Unpublished doctoral dissertation, University of California, Berkeley, 1978.

Sanders, J., and Nafziger, D.H. A basis for determining the adequacy of evaluation designs. *The Evaluation Center Occasional Paper Series*. Western Michigan University, Paper no, 4, 1975.

Scriven, M. Maximizing the Power of Causal Investigations: The Modus Operandi Method. In Popham, W.J. (Ed.), *Evaluation in Education*. Berkeley, CA: McCutcheon, 1975.

Scriven, M., and Roth, J. Needs assessment: Concept and Practice. *New Directions for Program Evaluation* 1:1–11, 1978.

Scriven, M., and Ward, J. (Eds.). *Evaluation News #2*. Berkeley, CA: McCutcheon, 1975.

Scriven, M., and Ward, J. (Eds.). *Evaluation News #3*. Berkeley, McCutcheon, 1976.

Shaw, M.E., and Wright, J.M. *Scales for the Measurement of Attitudes*. New York: McGraw-Hill, 1967.

Smith, D.M., and Smith, N.L. *Writing Effective Evaluation Reports*. Portland, OR: Northwest Regional Educational Laboratory, March, 1980.

Spear, M. Practical Charting Technique. New York: McGraw Hill, 1979.

Stufflebeam, D.L. Meta evaluation: An overview. *Evaluation and the Health Professions* 1(1):1978.

Stufflebeam, D.L. Working Paper on Needs Assessment in Evaluation. Paper presented at the First Annual Educational Research Association Topical Conference on Evaluation, San Francisco, California, 1977.

Stufflebeam, D.L. *Philosophical, Conceptual, and Practical Guides for Evaluating Education*. Kalamazoo, MI: Western Michigan University, 1978.

Suarey, T. *Needs Assessment for Technical Assistance: A Conceptual Overview and Comparison of Three Strategies*. Unpublished doctoral dissertation, Western Michigan University, 1980.

Sudman, S. *Applied Sampling*. New York: Academic, 1976.

Thurston, P. Revitalizing adversary evaluations: Deep dark deficitis or muddle mistaken musings. *Educational Researcher* 7(7):3–8, 1978.

University of Kentucky. College of Education. Bureau of School Service Study Team. *Research Procedures for Comprehensive Educational Planning: Curriculum and Instructional Practices*.

U.S. Department of Health, Education, and Welfare. Office of the Assistant Secretary for Planning and Evaluation. Office of Program Systems. *Needs Assessment: A Critical Perspective*, December 1977.

Webb, E.J., Campbell, D.T., Schwartz, R.D., and Sechrest, L. *Unobtrusive Measures: Nonreactive Research in the Social Sciences*. Chicago: Rand McNally, 1966.

Werner, L.K. *A Statewide Conceptual Framework for Local District Needs Assessment: The Illinois Problems Index*. Illinois Dept. of Ed. Springfield, IL: 1980.

Windle, C.D., Rosen, B.M., Goldsmith, H.F., and Shambaugh, J.P. A Demographic System for Comparative Assessment of Needs for Mental Health Services. *Resource Materials for Community Mental Health Program Evaluation (2nd ed.)*. 1977.

Wolf, R.L., and Arnstein, G. Trial by jury: A new evaluation method. *Phi Delta Kappan* 57(3):185–190, 1975.

# Index